LEARNING RESOURCES CTR/NEW ENGLAND TECH.
GEN   PR2774.A2 1986
Shakespeare,   Shakespeare's women :

3 0147 0001 0886 3

PR2774 .A

 W9-DAM-708

Shakespeare, William, 1564-1616.

Shakespeare's women

SHAKESPEARE'S WOMEN

A Playscript for Performance and Analysis

Libby Appel and Michael Flachmann

SOUTHERN ILLINOIS UNIVERSITY PRESS
Carbondale and Edwardsville

Copyright © 1986 by the Board of Trustees,
    Southern Illinois University
All rights reserved
Printed in the United States of America
Edited by Teresa White
Designed by Frank O. Williams, after design for
    Shakespeare's Lovers by Bob Nance

Library of Congress Cataloging in Publication Data

Shakespeare, William, 1564–1616.
    Shakespeare's women.

    Bibliography: p.
    1. Women—Drama. I. Appel, Libby, 1937– .
II. Flachmann, Michael, 1942– . III. Title.
PR2774.A2 1986   882.3'3   85-10859
ISBN 0-8093-1241-7

CAUTION Professionals and amateurs are
hereby warned that this play, being fully protected under the copyright law of the United
States of America, the British Empire, including
the dominion of Canada, and other countries of
the copyright union, is subject to royalties; and
anyone presenting this play without the consent
of the copyright holder will be liable to the pen-
alties by law provided. All applications for the
right of amateur or professional productions
must be made to the Director, Southern Illinois
University Press, Carbondale, IL 62902-3697.

TO TWO VERY INFLUENTIAL WOMEN
IN OUR LIVES AND WORK
SANDRA SINGER AND KIM FLACHMANN

Contents

Acknowledgments

WE ARE GRATEFUL to the many people whose support and encouragement have enabled us to complete this book in timely fashion: for suggestions and reviews of the manuscript, Susan Appel, Paul Appel, Kim Flachmann, Andrew Griggs, Elizabeth Gordon, Jim Holmes, and Sally Brown; for videotaping the first production, James Mangold; for photographs, Phillip Beck; for assistance in typing the manuscript, Terry Hansen, Judy Hachey, and Debbie Domingos; for editing the manuscript, Teresa White; for musical composition, Richard Babcock; for compassion and understanding, Christopher Flachmann; and for inspiration, creative energy, and commitment, the CalArts Theatre Company.

Introduction

Shakespeare's Women is like our first book, *Shakespeare's Lovers,* in that it serves both as a script for performance and as a play text for use in high school and college-level theater and English literature classes. As a play intended for performance, *Shakespeare's Women* is a unique and self-contained script that brings together a highly theatrical combination of scenes displaying Shakespeare's complex and intriguing view of women during the Renaissance. Two narrators, a man and a woman, introduce and comment upon these scenes, weaving together the different characters and situations into an original dramatic "tapestry" featuring such admired Shakespearean heroines as Rosalind, Viola, Lady Macbeth, Cleopatra, Kate, Juliet, Portia, Beatrice, and many others. The play is divided into two acts, with a total running time of approximately two hours; it involves between eight to twelve actors and requires the use of a simple set and minimal props. The primary attention of the script is focused upon the interrelationships of these characters within this newly created dramatic narrative.

Used in the classroom, *Shakespeare's Women* proceeds from our belief that Shakespeare's plays are best approached as scripts intended for performance, rather than as dry literary manuscripts excerpted from their proper theatrical milieu. In theater courses, the text may be used for scene study and in-class acting exercises, providing students with the opportunity to concentrate on individual scenes set apart from the larger, more intricate context of an entire Shakespearean play. In English classes, the play text may be used to introduce students to the different types of Renaissance women created by Shakespeare. In writing *Shakespeare's Women,* we have brought together our experience from the worlds of both theater and literature, and we are hopeful that this combined approach will encourage students and teachers from these complementary disciplines to work together in exploring Shakespeare's plays. In fact, the book's subtitle, *A Playscript for Performance and Analysis,* deliberately highlights these two important and interdependent uses of *Shakespeare's Women.*

The textual apparatus is intended to illuminate both the theatrical and literary aspects of *Shakespeare's Women.* Suggested stage directions appear on separate pages facing each page of script, thereby creating a promptbook format, while brief glosses to the right of the text provide definitions of obscure terms and phrases. A set of production notes offers further advice on staging, composition of the ensemble, doubling patterns, costumes, and music. In addition, a Commentary section explains each scene within its original dramatic context. Appended are musical scores for both songs in the play plus a concise bibliography on the topic of women in Shakespeare's plays.

However *Shakespeare's Women* is used, we hope that your journey through these pages will be delightful and instructive, challenging and satisfying. The more we work together, the more we realize that Shakespeare's world beckons most invitingly to those students and teachers who shun rigid, parochial disciplines and rely instead on interdisciplinary approaches to open up the text. By bringing together the best efforts of theater and literature, we have attempted to present Shakespeare's women in "all their infinite variety." We're pleased to share this brave and exciting new world with you.

Production Notes

Staging

THE ACTION OF THE PLAY takes place in the foyer or main lobby outside an elegant ballroom. A champagne supper and formal dance are taking place offstage. The various stage exits should presumably lead to the restrooms, cloakroom, the outside exit, and the ballroom.

The room should have a circular shape, with cantilevered platforms at different levels ringing the back half of the circle—perhaps as if the stage were the sunken lobby of a magnificent hotel. From the highest point up center, a four- or five-step stair unit leads down onto the stage.

The stage should be set with a few ornate French chairs. The fourth wall, between the actors and the audience, should seem as if it were entirely mirrored. When using this fourth wall, the actors must maintain the illusion that the stage is round. A large ashtray on a stand and two or three potted plants may be added to the sparse furnishings in the foyer.

The room is lit by a large, beautiful chandelier that hangs down from the center of the ceiling. The party begins early in the evening, and the play progresses from the beginning stages of the festivities, to the late hours of the night when people are tired and nerves are raw, and finally to the clear, bright light of morning as the dance ends and everyone goes home.

The Ensemble

ELEVEN ACTORS make up the ensemble: six women and five men. (This number could easily vary, depending upon the needs of a particular acting company.) Two main characters, a Male Narrator and a Female Narrator, contend with each other as they tell the story of this long night's party. These two Narrators play introductory, guiding, and observing roles in most of the scenes, but they will each take a significant role in two of the scenes.

The Male Narrator will become Leontes (from *The Winter's Tale*) in the final scene from act I, while the Female Narrator will be Cleopatra (from *Antony and Cleopatra*) toward the end of act II. In both cases, the assumption of these roles springs from the Narrators' needs to make each other and the rest of the ensemble understand their passionate points of view.

The roles in the remainder of the scenes may be divided according to the assembled talents of each individual acting company. In the original production of this script at California Institute of the Arts in the fall of 1984, the roles were carefully split among the actors to facilitate the development of an overall "through-line" of action for each member of the company. Therefore, although one actor may have had to play as many as eight separate roles, he or she maintained a logical (though sometimes zany) continuity of actions and emotions throughout the night. In this script, each scene puts the actor in different circumstances—a dramatic process that causes relationships and behavior to change accordingly. Based upon our conception of the continuity between similar characters, our suggested role distribution would be as follows:

> *First Woman:* Beatrice, Katherine, Hermione, Lady Macbeth, Duchess of York, and Charmian
> *Second Woman:* Margaret, Gertrude, Helena (*Midsummer Night's Dream*), Queen Elizabeth, and Emilia
> *Third Woman:* Hero, Isabella, Nerissa, Olivia, Ophelia, and Queen Margaret
> *Fourth Woman:* Ursula, Cordelia, Portia, Maria, Helena (*All's Well*), Lady (*Richard II*), and Desdemona
> *Fifth Woman:* Viola, Rosalind, Queen (*Richard II*), Juliet
>
> *First Man:* Iago, Proteus, Balthasar, Demetrius, Parolles, Maecenas, and Romeo

Second Man: Don Pedro, Hamlet, Baptista, Orsino, Sonnet
   130, and the Messenger *(Antony and Cleopatra)*
Third Man: Benedick, Egeus, Lear, Malvolio, Orlando, and
   Enobarbus
Fourth Man: Othello, Antonio, Kent, Claudio, Officer
   (Winter's Tale), Bertram, Macbeth, and Agrippa

No matter how these roles are distributed, every effort must be
made in a production to preserve the dramatic continuity of the action, the party environment, and the central conflict between the
men and the women. In other words, these should be treated not as
separate scenes from Shakespeare but as a sequential series of
events that work together as a unique dramatic narrative.

Costumes

ALL THE ACTORS wear modern evening clothes, as if they were
dressed elegantly for a contemporary formal dance. Styles will vary
according to individual tastes and the overall through-line of each
actor. Some women may be in long gowns, some in shorter ones,
and one or two in evening pants. The men's evening wear can range
from white or black tux jackets to formal tails. The Narrators are
dressed most beautifully: she should look tasteful, sophisticated,
and perhaps a bit slinky; he should be dashing, with a flower in the
lapel of his tuxedo. The clothes will not change for act II or for any
of the different characters that each actor plays. Accessories may be
removed as the evening wears on, and the second act in particular
will need to show the characters in various states of eerie, late-night
disarray, with ties untied, jackets off, and ladies' high heels removed
whenever appropriate. For example, the woman who plays Viola,
Rosalind, the Queen (from *Richard II*), and Juliet would be wearing
a man's tuxedo and a cap in her earlier masculine roles; later, when
in the course of the play she is revealed as a woman, she can take
off her jacket, cap, and tie, open her shirt at the neck, and roll up
her sleeves for her final scene as Juliet.

Music and the Musicians

THE MUSIC for the two songs from *Twelfth Night* and *Othello* may
be entirely drawn from English Renaissance scores (see Music sec-

tion). We suggest, however, that the dance music at the party have a contemporary style and beat (even if Renaissance tunes form the melodic base). In the original production of *Shakespeare's Women*, jazz worked splendidly as a musical motif. Our composer used some Renaissance melodies, in addition, as original music arranged for saxophone, flute, guitar, and percussion. This music subtly suggested the not-too-distant past, the 1940s and 1950s, while still underscoring both the contemporary and the sixteenth-century quality of the script. Party music is played offstage under much of the initial action, and it returns intermittently throughout the play when needed to underscore the action or to provide an ironic counterpoint.

Obtaining the original score. A score of the original music composed by Richard Babcock for the first production of *Shakespeare's Women* may be obtained from Southern Illinois University Press upon request.

The Promptbook Format

LIKE *Shakespeare's Lovers,* this play has been designed as a director's/actor's promptbook. The titles of the major scenes and sonnets are identified on the far right-hand pages, which also include the playscript, glossary definitions, and footnotes. The suggested stage directions on the left-hand facing pages serve as a skeletal outline for movement and action. Directors and actors will wish to write additional stage blocking, along with character objectives and actions, on these left-hand pages as character development is discovered and explored during the rehearsal process.

Scene Citations

WE STRONGLY RECOMMEND that producers of *Shakespeare's Women* refrain in performance from attempting to identify the individual scenes from Shakespearean plays. A list of the plays can be provided in the printed programs, perhaps accompanied by a message similar to the following: "The scenes and sonnets are listed here to satisfy your curiosity. Although all words and phrases in this play are from Shakespeare's own works, they have been woven together here to form a unique, individual entertainment. Prior knowledge of the plays is an unnecessary luxury. We hope you can enjoy this play for its own value." This script works so well on its own that scene announcements become a distraction, rather than a comfort, to the audiences.

The Text

THE ENTIRE TEXT of *Shakespeare's Women* has been newly edited from the most authoritative manuscripts extant. The 1623 First Folio served as the copy text for most selections, though scenes taken from the following plays are indebted to earlier sources: *Romeo and Juliet* (the Second Quarto of 1599), *The Merchant of Venice* (the First Quarto of 1600), *Hamlet* (the Second Quarto of 1604–5), *A Midsummer Night's Dream* (Q1 of 1600), Sonnets 61 and 130 (the Quarto of 1609), and *Richard II* (Q1 of 1597). Spelling and punctuation have been modernized and standardized throughout. Final decisions on all textual "accidentals" were made during the rehearsal process prior to the first production of *Shakespeare's Women;* as a result, every effort has been made to ensure that the spelling and punctuation in this script provide actors with a clear, comprehensible pattern for performance. Actors would do well, however, to consult folio and quarto editions of each of their scenes, since the original punctuation may yield helpful acting clues. In footnoting obscure words and phrases, the authors have relied upon *The Oxford English Dictionary* and other general reference works. Specific scenes have been identified in brackets in the text, though no attempt has been made to mention which words, phrases, and lines have been omitted within those scenes.

Shakespeare's Women was first presented on October 11, 1984, by the CalArts Theatre Company at the California Institute of the Arts (Valencia, California). It was directed by Libby Appel; Michael Flachmann was dramaturge; music was composed and directed by Richard Babcock; and the stage manager was Lars Petersen.

The cast in order of speaking appearance was as follows:

Stan Dodd	Male Narrator, Leontes
Carlton Miller	Female Narrator, Cleopatra
Jim Holmes	Benedick, Egeus, Lear, Petruchio, Malvolio, Orlando, and Enobarbus
Lynda Harvey	Beatrice, Katherina, Hermione, Lady Macbeth, Duchess of York, Charmian
Craig Cavanah	Othello, Antonio, Kent, Claudio, Officer, Bertram, Macbeth, Agrippa
Jay Michael Fraley	Iago, Balthasar, Demetrius, Parolles, Maecenas, Romeo
Gerald Ollison	Hamlet, Don Pedro, Baptista, Orsino, Messenger, Sonnet 130
Theresa Pugh	Hero, Isabella, Nerissa, Olivia, Ophelia, Queen Margaret
Vicki Thompson	Margaret, Gertrude Helena (*Dream*), Queen Elizabeth, Emilia
Diane Reynolds	Ursula, Cordelia, Portia, Maria, Helena (*All's Well*), the Lady (*Richard II*), Desdemona
Sally Brown	Viola, Rosalind, the Queen (*Richard II*), Juliet
Musicians	Richard Babcock—Woodwinds Peter Fagiola—Percussion Gary Rich—Guitar

The entire play takes place in the foyer of an adjacent ballroom. Party sounds and lively music can be heard offstage. Though orchestration and instruments are contemporary, the music has a distinctly Renaissance flavor. The stage is dimly lit with a lush, candlelight feeling.

The Male Narrator enters from stage left and crosses toward stage right. The Female Narrator enters from stage right and is heading toward stage left, to the offstage ladies' room. They meet at stage center. He has obviously been looking for a woman to pick up all night, and he speaks with her.

Act I
Frailty, Thy Name Is Woman

MALE NARRATOR
Did not I dance with you in Brabant once?

FEMALE NARRATOR
Did not I dance with you in Brabant once?

MALE NARRATOR
I know you did.

FEMALE NARRATOR
        How needless was it then
To ask the question?

MALE NARRATOR
          You must not be so quick.

FEMALE NARRATOR
'Tis long of you that spur me with such questions.

MALE NARRATOR
Your wit's too hot: it speeds too fast, 'twill tire.

FEMALE NARRATOR
Not till it leaves the rider in the mire.

MALE NARRATOR
What time o'day?

FEMALE NARRATOR
        The hour that fools should ask.

MALE NARRATOR
Now fair befall your mask!

FEMALE NARRATOR
Fair fall the face it covers!

MALE NARRATOR
And send you many lovers!

Brabant: a duchy now divided between Belgium and the Netherlands.

5

quick: sharp tongued.

'Tis long of you that spur me: It is because you are irritating me (with such questions).

10

fair befall: good luck to.

fall: befall.

The Female Narrator moves off left, laughing at the encounter. The Male Narrator is about to exit off right when Beatrice comes onstage center and stops down center in front of the fourth-wall mirrors to powder her nose.

The Male Narrator starts toward Beatrice with the intention of talking with her, but he is intercepted by Benedick, who pulls him off to the left and tells him his troubles. Benedick whispers, as he does not want to be overheard by Beatrice.

The Male Narrator is eyeing Beatrice lustfully, but he cannot leave while Benedick is busy railing against her. Beatrice finishes her primping and starts back to the party (stage right). Benedick storms off stage right, leaving the Male Narrator alone. Two beautiful women pass from stage right on their way to stage left exit, chattering excitedly about the party. The Male Narrator is happy to see them and heads in their direction. The women laugh at him and walk off left. The Narrator, feeling rejected and humiliated, sits down on one of the lobby chairs. Othello enters, reeling backward in pain and followed closely by Iago. The Male Narrator eavesdrops on their heated conversation.

FEMALE NARRATOR
Amen, so you be none!   15

MALE NARRATOR
Nay, then will I be gone.

BENEDICK
O, she misused me past the endurance of a block! An oak but   *misused:* abused.
with one green leaf on it would have answered her. My very
visor began to assume life and scold with her. She told me, not   *visor:* mask.
                                                                      20
thinking I had been myself, that I was the Prince's jester, that I   *huddling:* piling. *impos-*
was duller than a great thaw, huddling jest upon jest with such   *sible conveyance:* unbeliev-
impossible conveyance upon me that I stood like a man at a   able skill. *a man at a mark:*
mark, with a whole army shooting at me. She speaks poniards,   the center of a target. *pon-*
and every word stabs. If her breath were as terrible as her ter-   *iards:* daggers. *the North*
minations, there were no living near her—she would infect the   *Star:* i.e., the most distant
North Star. I would not marry her, though she were endowed   place imaginable. *had*
with all that Adam had left him before he transgressed. She   *left him:* had been left for
would have made Hercules have turned spit, yea, and have cleft   Adam by God. *cleft his*
his club to make the fire, too. Come, talk not of her. You shall   *club:* splintered Hercules'
find her the infernal Ate in good apparel. I would to God some   famous club and turned it
scholar would conjure her; for certainly, while she is here, a man   to firewood.
may live as quiet in hell as in a sanctuary, and people sin upon
purpose, because they would go thither. So indeed all disquiet,   *perturbation:* disruption,
horror, and perturbation follows her.   chaos.

OTHELLO
O, Iago!   35

IAGO
And did you see the handkerchief?

OTHELLO
Was that mine?

IAGO
Yours, by this hand. And to see how he prizes the foolish   *by this hand:* i.e., I'm tell-

---

17 *past the endurance of a block:* (she abused me) more than a block or tree or other senseless object could have
endured.

20 *the Prince's jester:* Don Pedro, Prince of Arragon (cf. *Much Ado about Nothing,* II.i).

21 *duller than a great thaw:* as dull as being forced to stay at home while the roads are muddy and impassable (or,
perhaps, as dull as watching ice melt).

24–25 *terminations:* the terms and expressions she uses (with a pun on the "endings" of relationships).

28 *made Hercules have turned spit:* turning the spit over a fire was considered a menial, demeaning kitchen duty.
The mythical reference is to the Amazonian warrior Omphale, who captured Hercules and forced him to wear women's
clothing and spin wool.

30 *the infernal Ate:* Greek goddess of discord (though Beatrice, unlike Ate, will wear good clothes).

30–31 *some scholar would conjure her:* scholars, like the legendary Dr. Faustus, reputedly had the power to call
forth and control evil spirits.

32 *live as quiet in hell:* i.e., hell would be a quiet place compared to her endless chatter here on earth.

Othello starts back to the party to find Desdemona.

Iago stops him.

Othello storms off in a great fury. At the same time, a beautiful woman is moving from stage left to stage right. As the Male Narrator approaches her, Iago steps toward her and escorts her up center to the party. Feeling disgruntled and lonely, the Male Narrator shuffles up center, hands in his pockets. He is met there by Egeus.

Before Egeus can finish his complaint, Hamlet crosses the stage.

woman, your wife! She gave it him, and he hath given it his whore.

OTHELLO
I would have him nine years a-killing. A fine woman! A fair woman! A sweet woman!

IAGO
Nay, you must forget that.

OTHELLO
Ay, let her rot, and perish, and be damned tonight, for she shall not live. No, my heart is turned to stone: I strike it, and it hurts my hand. O, the world hath not a sweeter creature! She might lie by an emperor's side and command him tasks.

IAGO
Nay, that's not your way.

OTHELLO
Hang her! I do but say what she is. So delicate with her needle! An admirable musician! Oh, she will sing the savageness out of a bear. Of so high and plenteous wit and invention.

IAGO
She's the worse for all this.

OTHELLO
O, a thousand, a thousand times! And then of so gentle a condition!

IAGO
Ay, too gentle.

OTHELLO
Nay, that's certain. But yet the pity of it, Iago. O Iago, the pity of it, Iago.

IAGO
If you are so fond over her iniquity, give her patent to offend; for if it touch not you, it comes near nobody.

OTHELLO
I will chop her into messes. Cuckold me!

MALE NARRATOR
Good Egeus, what's the news with thee?

EGEUS
Full of vexation come I, with complaint
Against my child, my daughter, Hermia.

HAMLET
O most pernicious woman!

ing the truth. *the foolish woman:* Othello's wife, Desdemona. *his whore:* Bianca, Cassio's mistress.

45

50

55

so fond over her iniquity: so foolish as to condone her wickedness. *patent:* license. *chop her into messes:* cut her into small portions.

vexation: anger.

---

60 *Cuckold:* the husband of an unfaithful wife was commonly referred to as a "cuckold" (often signified in art and literature of the period by symbolic horns on his head).

Proteus crosses in the opposite direction of Hamlet.

Bombarded by the complaints of all these unhappy men, the Male Narrator turns to the audience, shakes his head in consternation, and shrugs his shoulders. As he is about to exit stage left and leave the party entirely, he meets the Female Narrator, who is returning from the ladies' room. He does not remember her as the same woman he spoke with earlier, and he tries to pick her up again with the same line. As she begins to reply, they both recognize each other. She is angry, he embarrassed. She sees the look on his face and smiles. Music from the other room becomes louder now, and the lights dim up as if the party is expanding into this foyer. Several other couples enter, dancing. The music is upbeat—a jitterbug tempo.

Hero and Don Pedro step aside into the background. Margaret and Balthasar dance into center stage. She is clearly trying to get rid of him, and he persistently continues dancing with her.

O villain, villain, smiling damned villain! 65

PROTEUS
Thou, Julia, thou hast metamorphised me,
Made me neglect my studies, lose my time,
War with good counsel, set the world at naught, *War with good counsel:*
Made wit with musing weak, heart sick with thought. Ignore sound advice. *set*
the world at naught: care
MALE NARRATOR nothing for the world.
Did not I dance with you in Brabant once?

FEMALE NARRATOR
Did not I . . .

DON PEDRO
Lady, will you walk about with your friend?

HERO
So you walk softly and look sweetly and say nothing, *so:* only if.
I am yours for the walk—and especially when I walk away.

DON PEDRO
With me in your company? 75

HERO
I may say so, when I please.

DON PEDRO
And when please you to say so?

HERO
When I like your favor. *favor:* facial features.

DON PEDRO
Speak low, if you speak love.

BALTHASAR
Well, I would you did like me. *I would:* I wish.

MARGARET
So would not I, for your own sake. For I have many ill quali-
ties.

BALTHASAR
Which is one?

MARGARET
I say my prayers aloud.

BALTHASAR
I love you the better. The hearers may cry "Amen." 85

MARGARET
God match me with a good dancer!

BALTHASAR
Amen.

---

66 *metamorphised:* changed my personality totally (cf. Ovid's *Metamorphosis*).
69 *Made wit with musing weak:* i.e., Proteus has enfeebled his wit by brooding over his love for Julia.

Margaret walks off with Balthasar doggedly following her. Ursula and Antonio dance into center stage. Antonio is looking around for another woman, while Margaret is trying to capture his attention. He continues to dance with her unwillingly.

Ursula and Antonio dance into the background, while Beatrice and Benedick dance to center stage. He is holding her close, cheek-to-cheek. She is trying to maintain some distance between them.

MARGARET
And God keep him out of my sight when the dance is done.
Answer, clerk.
BALTHASAR
No more words. The clerk is answered.   90
URSULA
I know you well enough. You are Signior Antonio.
ANTONIO
At a word, I am not.
URSULA
I know you by the waggling of your head.
ANTONIO
To tell you true, I counterfeit him.
URSULA
You could never do him so ill-well, unless you were the very
man. Here's his dry hand, up and down. You are he, you are he.
ANTONIO
At a word, I am not.
URSULA
Come, come, do you think I do not know you by your excellent
wit? Can virtue hide itself? Go to, mum; you are he. Graces will
appear, and there's an end.
BEATRICE
Will you not tell me who told you so?
BENEDICK
No, you shall pardon me.
BEATRICE
Nor will you not tell me who you are?
BENEDICK
Not now.
BEATRICE
That I was disdainful—well, this was Signior Benedick that said   105
so.
BENEDICK
What's he?
BEATRICE
I am sure you know him well enough.
BENEDICK
Not I, believe me.

do him so ill-well: imitate his silly mannerisms so exactly. *dry hand:* a sign of old age. *up and down:* a perfect copy (with a pun on shaking hands up and down). *mum:* be silent. *and there's an end:* there's no more to be said about the matter.

---

89 *Answer, clerk:* Balthasar, like a good parish clerk responding to a litany of prayers, has been saying "Amen." Margaret is simply calling for his next answer in this witty dialogue.

Beatrice walks off, leaving Benedick at stage center. He gazes after her, then follows forlornly. The other couples dance back offstage to the party inside. The Narrators, who have each been watching the dancers from opposite sides of the stage, come together down center and talk.

The Female Narrator sits down on a lobby chair and faces upstage, as if she is part of the audience. King Lear enters with Kent, proud and excited to show off his favorite daughter. Cordelia follows reluctantly behind, nervous and embarrassed. The Male Narrator points out these three to the Female Narrator, then steps aside to watch the scene.

BEATRICE
Did he never make you laugh?   110

BENEDICK
I pray you, what is he?

BEATRICE
Why, he is the Prince's jester, a very dull fool. Only his gift is in devising impossible slanders. None but libertines delight in him; and the commendation is not in his wit, but in his villainy, for he both pleases men and angers them, and then they laugh at him and beat him. I am sure he is in the fleet. I would he had boarded me.

BENEDICK
When I know the gentleman, I'll tell him what you say.

BEATRICE
Do, do. We must follow the leaders.

BENEDICK
In every good thing.

BEATRICE
Nay, if they lead to any ill, I will leave them at the next turning.

MALE NARRATOR
I thank God I am not a woman, to be touched with so many giddy offenses.

FEMALE NARRATOR
If you were man, as man you are in show,
You would not use a gentle lady so.

MALE NARRATOR
That a woman conceived me, I thank her.

FEMALE NARRATOR
How vexest thou this man! Talkest thou nothing but of ladies?

MALE NARRATOR
Women!
A woman moved is like a fountain troubled:
Muddy, ill-seeming, thick, bereft of beauty.
Her life is bound in shallows and in miseries.
I'll show you the manner of it.

FEMALE NARRATOR
Indeed! Ay, indeed!

MALE NARRATOR
It is a wise father that knows his own child.

Prince: Don Pedro (cf. line 20 in this scene). *Only his gift:* His only skill. *impossible:* incredible, not to be believed. *libertines:* those who lead a wild and dissolute life. *villainy:* his compulsion to make fun of other people. *fleet:* company of soldiers. *know:* meet, become acquainted with. *the leaders:* the leaders of the dance.

the next turning: the next turn in the dance.

touched: infected, tainted.

in show: in outward appearance.

conceived: gave birth to.

moved: angry (like muddy, swirling water). *bereft:* deprived.

---

117 *boarded:* encountered in a battle of wits (with, no doubt, a sexual pun). Beatrice continues the nautical metaphor begun with the word "fleet" (line 116).

131 *bound in shallows:* like a ship stuck on a sandbar, unable to break free.

Kent sets up a chair for Lear at stage center.

Lear laughs a little to cover his rising anger.

How sharper than a serpent's tooth it is   135
To have a thankless child.

[*King Lear*, I.i]

LEAR

          Now, our joy,
Although our last and least, to whose young love   *least:* Cordelia was Lear's
The vines of France and milk of Burgundy   youngest daughter. *vines:*
Strive to be interessed, what can you say to draw   vineyards. *milk:* rich pas-
A third more opulent than your sisters? Speak.   tures. *Strive to be inter-*
CORDELIA   *essed:* Vie for ownership or
Nothing, my lord.   possession. *draw:* win.
LEAR   *opulent:* rich, valuable.
Nothing?
CORDELIA
Nothing.
LEAR
Nothing will come of nothing. Speak again.
CORDELIA
Unhappy that I am, I cannot heave   10
My heart into my mouth. I love your majesty
According to my bond, no more nor less.   *bond:* duty as a daughter.
LEAR
How, how, Cordelia? Mend your speech a little,
Lest you may mar your fortunes.
CORDELIA
          Good my lord,   15
You have begot me, bred me, loved me. I
Return those duties back as are right fit: *right fit:* proper.
Obey you, love you, and most honor you.
Why have my sisters husbands, if they say
They love you all? Happily, when I shall wed,   *Happily:* As is appropriate.
That lord whose hand must take my plight shall carry   *plight:* pledge (marriage
Half my love with him, half my care and duty.   vows).
Sure I shall never marry like my sisters,
To love my father all.
LEAR
But goes thy heart with this?   25

---

9 *Nothing will come of nothing:* the phrase is an echo of Aristotle's famous "Ex nihilo nihil fit."
10–11 *I cannot . . . mouth:* I have difficulty expressing my innermost thoughts and emotions in words.

Cordelia kneels before Lear.

Lear stands, then circles Cordelia, angrily denouncing her.

The Male Narrator admonishes Cordelia as she retreats. He then turns to the Female Narrator with his question.

The Female Narrator leads Cordelia offstage.

Hamlet walks by and speaks to the Female Narrator as she is returning from comforting Cordelia. He is elegantly dressed, drinking from a champagne glass. In spite of his teasing, casual manner, one can sense great anger lurking beneath his surface appearance.

CORDELIA

        Ay, my good lord.

LEAR

So young and so untender?

CORDELIA

So young, my lord, and true.

LEAR

Let it be so: Thy truth then be thy dower.   *dower:* dowry.

For, by the sacred radiance of the sun,   30

The mysteries of Hecate and the night,   *Hecate:* goddess of witch-

By all the operation of the orbs   craft and the moon. *opera-*

From whom we do exist and cease to be,   *tion of the orbs:* the

Here I disclaim all my paternal care,   astrological influence of the

Propinquity, and property of blood,   stars. *Propinquity, and*

And as a stranger to my heart and me   *property of blood:* Filial

Hold thee from this for ever. The barbarous Scythian,   intimacy and kinship. *from*

Or he that makes his generation messes   *this:* from this time for-

To gorge his appetite, shall to my bosom   ward. *makes his generation*

Be as well neighbored, pitied, and relieved   *messes:* feeds on his own

As thou my sometime daughter.   children. *sometime:* former.

KENT

        Good my Liege—

LEAR

Peace, Kent!

Come not between the dragon and his wrath.   *his wrath:* the object of his

I loved her most, and thought to set my rest   anger (i.e., Cordelia).

On her kind nursery. Hence, and avoid my sight.   *avoid:* leave.

So be my grave my peace, as here I give   *give:* take.

Her father's heart from her.

MALE NARRATOR

To you your father should be as a god.

Can you love this lady?   50

FEMALE NARRATOR

Nay, ask me if I can refrain from love.

HAMLET

How cheerfully my mother looks, and my father died within
these two hours.

---

37 *Scythian:* an ancient race of people infamous for their savagery.

45–46 *set my rest . . . nursery:* spend my declining years resting in her care. "Set my rest" was a term from card
games meaning "to stake everything" on one hand (i.e., the "rest" of one's money).

47 *So be my grave my peace:* Since I can not obtain peace living with Cordelia, I will find it only in my grave.

Hamlet jokes with the Male Narrator.

The Male Narrator sees Gertrude entering and warns Hamlet.

Gertrude crosses to Hamlet, ready to berate him for his bad behavior.

Gertrude responds angrily.

Gertrude starts to exit. Hamlet grabs her arm and pulls her downstage center facing the fourth-wall mirror. He pulls a chair over and forces her to sit down.

FEMALE NARRATOR
Nay, 'tis twice two months, my lord.

HAMLET
So long? Nay, then, let the devil wear black, for I'll have a suit   55
of sables. O heavens, died two months ago and not forgotten
yet? Then there's hope a great man's memory may outlive his life
half a year!

MALE NARRATOR
The Queen, your mother, in most great affliction   *The Queen, your mother:*
Of spirit hath sent me to you. Poor wretch,   Gertrude, mother of Ham-
That for thy mother's fault art thus exposed   let and wife of Claudius.
To loss.

[*Hamlet,* III.iv]

HAMLET
Now, mother, what's the matter?

QUEEN
Hamlet, thou hast thy father much offended.   *thy father:* Hamlet's step-
                                                father, Claudius.
HAMLET
Mother, you have my father much offended.   *my father:* Old Hamlet,
                                             Gertrude's first husband
QUEEN   and young Hamlet's father.
Come, come, you answer with an idle tongue.   *idle:* foolish.

HAMLET
Go, go, you question with a wicked tongue.   5

QUEEN
Why, how now, Hamlet?

HAMLET
                    What's the matter now?

QUEEN
Have you forgot me?

HAMLET
                No, by the rood, not so: *rood:* cross.
You are the Queen, your husband's brother's wife,   10
And (would it were not so!) you are my mother.

QUEEN
Nay, then, I'll set those to you that can speak.

HAMLET
Come, come, and sit you down; you shall not budge.

55–56 *a suit of sables:* Hamlet jokingly offers to give his black mourning clothes to the devil in exchange for rich and luxurious furs.

Hamlet shows Gertrude his watch fob with a picture inside, then points to a locket around her neck.

You go not till I set you up a glass
Where you may see the inmost part of you.
QUEEN
What wilt thou do? Thou wilt not murder me?
HAMLET
Leave wringing of your hands. Peace! Sit you down
And let me wring your heart, for so I shall
If it be made of penetrable stuff,
If damned custom have not brazed it so
That it is proof and bulwark against sense.
QUEEN
What have I done that thou dar'st wag thy tongue
In noise so rude against me?
HAMLET
                              Such an act
That blurs the grace and blush of modesty,
Calls virtue "hypocrite," takes off the rose
From the fair forehead of an innocent love
And sets a blister there, makes marriage vows
As false as dicers' oaths. O, such a deed
As from the body of contraction plucks
The very soul, and sweet religion makes
A rhapsody of words.
QUEEN
                      Ay me, what act,
That roars so loud and thunders in the index?
HAMLET
Look here upon this picture, and on this,
The counterfeit presentment of two brothers.
See what a grace was seated on this brow:
Hyperion's curls, the front of Jove himself,
An eye like Mars, to threaten and command,
A station like the herald Mercury
New-lighted on a heaven-kissing hill—
A combination and form indeed,
Where every god did seem to set his seal,
To give the world assurance of a man.
This was your husband. Look you now, what follows:

glass: mirror.
15

damned custom: repeated sinful behavior. *brazed:* hardened (literally, plated over with brass). *dar'st:* darest (dare to).

25

dicers' oaths: pledges sworn by men playing dice. *contraction:* the marriage contract. *religion:* religious vows. *rhapsody:* meaningless medley.
index: table of contents of a book.
35
counterfeit presentment: painted representation. *two brothers:* Hamlet's father and Hamlet's uncle, Claudius. *Hyperion:* the beautiful sun god of Greek mythology. *front:* forehead. *Mars:* Roman god of war. *station:* stance, bearing. *Mercury:* Roman messen-

21 *proof and bulwark against sense:* armor and fortification that keep out your natural emotions.
26–28 *takes off the rose . . . there:* replaces the rose, symbol of romantic love, with a venereal blister, mark of a whore.

Hamlet grabs Gertrude's locket and tears it from her neck.

Hamlet tries to recover his calm exterior and walks toward the Male Narrator, laughing.

Hamlet rushes back to Gertrude and forces her to look into the mirror.

Gertrude tries to avert her eyes from the mirror.

Hamlet remains behind her, whispering in her ear, urging her to look inside her very soul.

Gertrude rises and starts to leave. Hamlet follows her, unrelenting in his fury.

Hamlet continues whispering angrily in her ear as she tries to hurry offstage.

Here is your husband, like a mildewed ear,
Blasting his wholesome brother. Have you eyes?
Could you on this fair mountain leave to feed,
And batten on this moor? Ha, have you eyes?
You cannot call it love, for at your age
The heyday in the blood is tame, it's humble,
And waits upon the judgment. And what judgment
Would step from this to this? What devil was't
That thus hath cozened you at hoodman-blind?
O shame! Where is thy blush? Rebellious hell,
If thou canst mutine in a matron's bones,
To flaming youth let virtue be as wax
And melt in her own fire. Proclaim no shame
When the compulsive ardor gives the charge,
Since frost itself as actively doth burn,
And reason pandars will.

QUEEN
                    O Hamlet, speak no more!
Thou turn'st mine eyes into my very soul,
And there I see such black and grained spots
As will not leave their tinct.

HAMLET
                    Nay, but to live
In the rank sweat of an enseamed bed,
Stewed in corruption, honeying and making love
Over the nasty sty—

QUEEN
                    O, speak to me no more!
These words, like daggers, enter in mine ears.
No more, sweet Hamlet!

HAMLET
                    A murderer and a villain!
A slave that is not twentieth part the tithe
Of your precedent lord. A vice of kings,
A cutpurse of the empire and the rule,
That from a shelf the precious diadem stole
And put it in his pocket—

QUEEN
            No more!

---

ger of the gods. New-lighted: Just landed. *assurance:* a perfect example. *husband:* i.e., your new husband, Claudius. *ear:* of grain. *Blasting:* Infecting, corrupting. *this fair mountain:* Old Hamlet. *batten:* gorge yourself. *this moor:* Claudius. *heyday:* sexual excitement.

from this to this: from your former husband to your present one. *cozened:* cheated, tricked. *hoodman-blind:* blindman's bluff. *mutine:* mutiny. *compulsive ardor:* lustful behavior. *gives the charge:* begins the attack (military metaphor). *pandars: acts as a procurer for.*

grained: ingrained, indelible. *spots:* moral stains. *leave their tinct:* lose their color. *enseamed:* larded over with grease. *sty:* an enclosure or pen where pigs sleep. *tithe:* a tenth part. *precedent:* former (i.e., Old Hamlet). *cutpurse:* pickpocket, thief (implying that Claudius has stolen the throne). *diadem:* crown.

60–61 *Since . . . will:* Since the lustfulness of old age (normally a "frosty" time) burns just as brightly as youthful love, and reason, which should calm desire, does the reverse and encourages it. . . .

75 *vice:* clown or jester (with a reference to the Vice character of medieval morality plays).

As the Queen and Hamlet exit, the Male Narrator stands and calls after Gertrude.
As the Male Narrator speaks to the departing characters, Isabella enters and addresses him.
The Male Narrator takes two chairs, places them facing each other at stage center, and then introduces Isabella to the Female Narrator.

Claudio enters, champagne glass in hand, walks eagerly toward Isabella, and takes a seat opposite her. The Male Narrator stands upstage between the two, watching.

MALE NARRATOR
Relenting fool and shallow changing woman!　　　　　80
Thy mother's name is ominous to children.
ISABELLA
I have a brother is condemned to die.
MALE NARRATOR
Here, sister, armed in intent.

[*Measure for Measure*, III.i]

CLAUDIO
Now, sister, what's the comfort?
ISABELLA
　　　　　　　　Why,
As all comforts are: most good, most good indeed.
Lord Angelo, having affairs to heaven,
Intends you for his swift ambassador,
Where you shall be an everlasting leiger.
Therefore, your best appointment make with speed:
Tomorrow you set on.
CLAUDIO
　　　　　　Is there no remedy?
ISABELLA
None, but such remedy as, to save a head,
To cleave a heart in twain.
CLAUDIO
But is there any?
ISABELLA
　　　　　　Yes, brother, you may live.
There is a devilish mercy in the judge,
If you'll implore it, that will free your life,
But fetter you till death.
CLAUDIO
　　　　　　Perpetual durance?
ISABELLA
Ay, just; perpetual durance, a restraint,
though all the world's vastidity you had,
To a determined scope.

affairs to: business with.
　5
leiger: specially appointed
ambassador. *appointment:*
preparation. *set on:* begin
your journey (to heaven).

　10

　15
fetter: enchain, restrain.

durance: imprisonment.

just: exactly.

　20

10–11 *None . . . twain:* The only possible remedy to save your life would break my heart in two.

18–20 *a restraint . . . scope:* Even if you had the whole world to wander in, you would still feel restrained (by guilt over the immoral bargain you had made with the judge).

Claudio rises and paces.

Isabella reaches for Claudio's hand and grasps it.

CLAUDIO
               Let me know the point.

ISABELLA
O, I do fear thee, Claudio, and I quake,
Lest thou a fev'rous life shouldst entertain
And six or seven winters more respect
Than a perpetual honor. Dar'st thou die?
The sense of death is most in apprehension,
And the poor beetle that we tread upon
In corp'ral sufferance finds a pang as great
As when a giant dies.

CLAUDIO
              Why give you me this shame?
Think you I can a resolution fetch
From flow'ry tenderness? If I must die,
I will encounter darkness as a bride
And hug it in my arms.

ISABELLA
There spake my brother! There my father's grave
Did utter forth a voice! Yes, thou must die.
Thou art too noble to conserve a life
In base appliances. This outward-sainted deputy,
Whose settled visage and deliberate word
Nips youth in the head, and follies doth enew
As falcon doth the fowl, is yet a devil.
His filth within being cast, he would appear
A pond as deep as hell.

CLAUDIO
              The prenzie Angelo!

ISABELLA
O, 'tis the cunning livery of hell,
The damned'st body to invest and cover
In prenzie guards! Dost thou think, Claudio,
If I would yield him my virginity,
Thou mightst be freed!

---

entertain: cherish, desire.

25
apprehension: anticipation.

corp'ral sufferance: bodily pain. *pang:* a sharp attack of pain.
30
a resolution fetch: obtain strength of purpose.
flow'ry tenderness: comforting poetic phrases.

35

conserve: preserve, keep.
In base appliances: Through dishonorable means. *settled visage:* calm outward appearance.
cast: vomited up and/or analyzed.

prenzie: princely (?).

livery: clothing, outward show. *invest:* clothe.
guards: ornamental trimmings on clothes (with a pun on "military strength").

---

21 *Let me know the point:* Come directly to the point of what you have to say.

23–25 *Lest thou . . . honor:* I fear you would value six or seven extra years of uneasy, guilt-ridden life more than you would an honorable death.

40 *Nips youth in the head:* Strikes quickly from above, like a hawk or falcon swooping down on its prey.

40–41 *and follies . . . fowl:* the sense seems to be that Angelo, through his overzealous use of legal authority, pursues and punishes petty vices ("follies") with the same natural energy as a hawk chases its prey down into the water ("doth enew").

Claudio sits and faces Isabella, hoping she will sense his despair and free him from his death sentence.

Alarmed at Claudio's sudden reversal, Isabella starts to rise.

Claudio crosses to her and kneels, desperately trying to make her understand his fear.

CLAUDIO

          O heavens, it cannot be!   50

ISABELLA

Yes. He would give't thee, from this rank offense,
So to offend him still. This night's the time
That I should do what I abhor to name,
Or else thou diest tomorrow.

CLAUDIO

Thou shalt not do't.

ISABELLA

        O, were it but my life,
I'd throw it down for your deliverance
As frankly as a pin.

CLAUDIO

        Thanks, dear Isabel.

ISABELLA

Be ready, Claudio, for your death tomorrow.   60

CLAUDIO

Yes. Has he affections in him,
That thus can make him bite the law by the nose,
When he would force it? Sure, it is no sin.
Or of the deadly seven it is the least.

ISABELLA

Which is the least?   65

CLAUDIO

If it were damnable, he being so wise,
Why would he for the momentary trick
Be perdurably fined? O Isabel!

ISABELLA

What says my brother?

CLAUDIO

        Death is a fearful thing.   70

ISABELLA

And shamed life a hateful.

CLAUDIO

Ay, but to die, and go we know not where;
To lie in cold obstruction and to rot;
This sensible warm motion to become
A kneaded clod, and the delighted spirit
To bathe in fiery floods; or to reside

give't thee: give you your freedom. *from:* in return for. *So to offend him still:* To continue your own lustful behavior. *what I abhor to name:* i.e., make love with Angelo.

As frankly as a pin: As freely as I would throw down a pin.

affections: passions. *bite the law by the nose:* flout the law. *force:* enforce. *it is no sin:* i.e., making love with Angelo.

trick: trifle. *perdurably fined:* punished forever (in hell).

obstruction: death. *sensible:* capable of feeling. *kneaded:* shapeless. *delighted spirit:* eternal soul.

51 *rank offense:* lustful and offensive behavior (with a pun on Angelo's high social "rank").

Isabella turns away in disgust from the pleading Claudio.

Isabella crosses to exit stage left.

She turns to Claudio and pronounces her final judgment upon him.

Isabella exits. Claudio remains, abandoned and hopeless, then begins to exit slowly up right. The Male Narrator delivers his first line to the departing Isabella, then turns and addresses the women in the audience. He calms himself, then playfully apologizes to the women.

Turning to the Female Narrator, he feels triumphant in having displayed Isabella as an example of the cruelty of women.

In thrilling region of thick-ribbed ice;
To be imprisoned in the viewless winds
And blown with restless violence round about
The pendant world; or to be worse than worst
Of those that lawless and incertain thought
Imagine howling—'tis too horrible!
The weariest and most loathed worldly life
That age, ache, penury, and imprisonment
Can lay on nature is a paradise
To what we fear of death.

ISABELLA
Alas, alas.

CLAUDIO
　　　　Sweet sister, let me live.
What sin you do to save a brother's life,
Nature dispenses with the deed so far
That it becomes a virtue.

ISABELLA
　　　　O you beast!
O faithless coward! O dishonest wretch!
Wilt thou be made a man out of my vice?
Is't not a kind of incest, to take life
From thine own sister's shame? What should I think?
Heaven shield my mother played my father fair!
For such a warped slip of wilderness
Ne'er issued from his blood. Take my defiance!
Die! Perish! Might but my bending down
Reprieve thee from thy fate, it should proceed.
I'll pray a thousand prayers for thy death,
No word to save thee.

CLAUDIO
Nay, hear me, Isabel.

ISABELLA
　　　　O, fie, fie, fie!
Thy sin's not accidental, but a trade.
Mercy to thee would prove itself a bawd.
'Tis best that thou diest quickly.

MALE NARRATOR
Savage, extreme, rude, cruel, not to trust. Women: the weaker
vessels! By your leave, sweet ladies, I chance to talk a little wild.
Forgive me. How is it with you, lady?

fiery floods: the torments of hell. *thrilling:* i.e., able to make one shiver with cold. *viewless:* invisible. *pendant:* hanging in space (according to Ptolemaic theory). *lawless . . . thought:* fearful conjecture. *penury:* extreme poverty.

dispenses with: excuses.

95

a warped slip of wilderness: i.e., the "degenerate" Claudio. *defiance:* my rejection of your request. *it:* your execution.

105
trade: way of life.
prove itself a bawd: provide opportunity for further lustful behavior.

110

97 *Heaven . . . fair!:* Heaven defend my mother against the charge of infidelity!

The Female Narrator is obviously not convinced, so the Male Narrator prepares to present another example—the weakness of Helena.

Helena enters the lobby, searching for Demetrius, who soon appears dancing with a woman. His dancing partner is clearly not interested in him. As the departing Claudio passes, the woman gazes admiringly at him. Helena cuts in on Demetrius. The woman dashes off in the direction of Claudio, leaving Demetrius in Helena's arms. Furious at the situation, Demetrius tries to follow Claudio and the woman, but Helena stops him. He turns on her angrily.

Helena kneels and holds one of Demetrius' legs; she grabs his hand and forces him to pat her on the head.

Demetrius escapes from her grasp.

FEMALE NARRATOR
Alas, how is it with you?
MALE NARRATOR
Ay me, how weak a thing the heart of women is!
FEMALE NARRATOR
I pray you, let us see.

[A Midsummer Night's Dream, II.i]

DEMETRIUS
I love thee not; therefore, pursue me not.
Where is Lysander and fair Hermia?
The one I'll slay; the other slayeth me.
Thou told'st me they were stol'n unto this wood;
And here am I, and wode within this wood,
Because I cannot meet my Hermia.
Hence, get thee gone, and follow me no more!

wode: mad, crazy (with a pun on "wood").

HELENA
You draw me, you hard-hearted adamant.
But yet you draw not iron, for my heart
Is true as steel. Leave you your power to draw,
And I shall have no power to follow you.

draw: attract.
Leave you: Give up.

DEMETRIUS
Do I entice you? Do I speak you fair?
Or rather do I not in plainest truth
Tell you I do not nor I cannot love you?

HELENA
And even for that do I love you the more.
I am your spaniel; and, Demetrius,
The more you beat me, I will fawn on you.
Use me but as your spaniel—spurn me, strike me,
Neglect me, lose me—only give me leave,
Unworthy as I am, to follow you.
What worser place can I beg in your love
(And yet a place of high respect with me)
Than to be used as you use your dog?

15

leave: permission.
20

used . . . use: treated . . . treat.

DEMETRIUS
Tempt not too much the hatred of my spirit,
For I am sick when I do look on thee.

Tempt not: Do not put to the test. *the hatred of my*

---

8 *adamant:* lodestone or magnet (with a pun on "hard-hearted," since adamant was considered the hardest of all stones).

He takes a strong stance and warns her of danger.

As Helena stalks him, he moves backward, tripping over chairs left onstage from the preceding scene. Helena throws the chairs out of her way, pushes Demetrius to the ground, and sits on his chest, her knees straddling his body.

Demetrius rolls her over and ends up lying on top of her.

Demetrius escapes from her and exits stage right.

Helena recovers her breath, regains her dignity, and smooths her dress while looking into the fourth-wall mirror.

She runs off in the direction Demetrius has fled.

HELENA
And I am sick when I look not on you.

DEMETRIUS
You do impeach your modesty too much
To leave the city and commit yourself
Into the hands of one that loves you not;
To trust the opportunity of night
And the ill counsel of a desert place
With the rich worth of your virginity.

HELENA
Your virtue is my privilege. For that
It is not night when I do see your face,
Therefore I think I am not in the night;
Nor doth this wood lack worlds of company,
For you, in my respect, are all the world.
Then how can it be said I am alone,
When all the world is here to look on me?

DEMETRIUS
I'll run from thee and hide me in the brakes,
And leave thee to the mercy of wild beasts.

HELENA
The wildest hath not such a heart as you.
Run when you will. The story shall be changed:
Apollo flies, and Daphne holds the chase;
The dove pursues the griffin; the mild hind
Makes speed to catch the tiger—bootless speed,
When cowardice pursues and valor flies!

DEMETRIUS
I will not stay thy questions. Let me go!
Or if thou follow me, do not believe
But I shall do thee mischief in the wood.

HELENA
Ay, in the temple, in the town, the field,
You do me mischief. Fie, Demetrius!
Your wrongs do set a scandal on my sex.
We cannot fight for love, as men may do;
We should be wooed, and were not made to woo.
I'll follow thee, and make a heaven of hell,
To die upon the hand I love so well.

spirit: my hatred of you.

impeach: call into question.

30
ill counsel: untrustworthy nature. *desert:* deserted, solitary.
virtue: honorable nature. *privilege:* safeguard. *For that:* Since.

in my respect: as far as I am concerned.

brakes: bushes.

griffin: a fictitious monster with the head of an eagle and the body of a lion.
hind: female deer. *bootless:* useless. *stay thy questions:* wait here in conversation with you.

55

upon the hand: i.e., by

44 *Apollo . . . chase:* In the well-known classical myth, Daphne, fleeing from Apollo, was saved from rape by being changed into a laurel tree. Here, in Helena's revised myth, the woman pursues the man.

The Female Narrator finishes the Male Narrator's speech for him. Then she praises Helena's devotion to Demetrius, trying unsuccessfully to hide her own anger.

As the Narrators are talking, Katherina enters. She walks to the mirror, repairs her makeup, then props her leg up on the chair and straightens her stocking.

Petruchio enters, sees the beautiful Kate, and whispers in the Male Narrator's ear.

The Narrators sit down to observe the action.

Petruchio surprises Kate, who thought she was alone in the foyer. She sits in a chair up left with her back to this advancing wooer.

Petruchio is truly impressed by her beauty.

Kate rises from her chair.

MALE NARRATOR

               I never knew a woman
so dote upon a man: And she, sweet lady, dotes,
Devoutly dotes, dotes in idolatry—

FEMALE NARRATOR

Upon this spotted and inconstant man. For she's a woman to be
pitied much. Her sighs will make a batt'ry in his breast. I could
wish he would modestly examine himself to see how much he is
unworthy so good a lady.

MALE NARRATOR

Away with that audacious woman! And here's another. O, when
she is angry, she is keen and shrewd.

PETRUCHIO

Is she so hot a shrew as she's reported?

MALE NARRATOR

Be judge yourself.

dote upon: shower foolish
affection on.

spotted: morally stained.
batt'ry: wound (military
metaphor).

audacious: bold, insolent.

shrew: a hot-tempered,
troublesome, scolding
woman.

Demetrius' hand.

[*The Taming of the Shrew,* II.i]

PETRUCHIO

Good morrow, Kate, for that's your name, I hear.

KATHERINA

Well have you heard, but something hard of hearing.
They call me Katherine that do talk of me.

PETRUCHIO

You lie, in faith, for you are called plain Kate
And bonny Kate and sometimes Kate the curst;
But Kate, the prettiest Kate in Christendom,
Kate of Kate Hall, my super-dainty Kate,
For dainties are all Kates; and therefore, Kate,
Take this of me, Kate of my consolation:
Hearing thy mildness praised in every town,
Thy virtues spoke of, and thy beauty sounded
(Yet not so deeply as to thee belongs),
Myself am moved to woo thee for my wife.

KATHERINA

Moved? In good time! Let him that moved you hither
Remove you hence. I knew you at the first:
You were a moveable.

PETRUCHIO

          Why, what's a moveable?

KATHERINA

A joined-stool.

something: somewhat.

5

Kate Hall: i.e., the house
that Kate rules over. *dainties . . . Kates:* Petruchio
puns on "cates": delicacies,
sweetmeats. *of me:* from
me. *sounded:* proclaimed
(with a pun on "plumbed"
or "tested for depth"). *belongs:* is appropriate. *In
good time!:* Indeed!
moveable: a piece of furni-
ture easily moved.

joined-stool: a stool fitted

Petruchio quickly sits in the chair, grabs Kate by the arm, and pulls her down onto his lap.

She immediately escapes from his grasp, stands up, and walks away from him.

PETRUCHIO
       Thou hast hit it! Come, sit on me.
KATHERINA
Asses are made to bear, and so are you.
PETRUCHIO
Women are made to bear, and so are you.
KATHERINA
No such jade as you, if me you mean.
PETRUCHIO
Alas, good Kate, I will not burden thee,
For knowing thee to be but young and light.
KATHERINA
Too light for such a swain as you to catch,
And yet as heavy as my weight should be.
PETRUCHIO
Should be? Should—buzz!
KATHERINA
       Well ta'en, and like a buzzard.
PETRUCHIO
O slow-winged turtle, shall a buzzard take thee?
KATHERINA
Ay, for a turtle, as he takes a buzzard.
PETRUCHIO
Come, come, you wasp; in faith, you are too angry.
KATHERINA
If I be waspish, best beware my sting.
PETRUCHIO
My remedy is then to pluck it out.
KATHERINA
Ay, if the fool could find it where it lies.
PETRUCHIO
Who knows not where a wasp does wear his sting?
In his tail.
KATHERINA
In his tongue.
PETRUCHIO
Whose tongue?

or joined together with separate pieces of wood.
hit it: guessed correctly.
20

bear: carry (with a double pun on "childbirth" and "bearing the weight of a lover"). *jade:* an old, tired horse.

swain: young country lover. *catch:* attract as a lover (with a pun on "musical refrain"). *buzz:* the sound of a bee (playing on Kate's "as heavy as my weight should *be*"). *Well ta'en:* an ironic compliment here (e.g., Well, aren't you smart!). *take:* mistake/overtake. *wasp:* Petruchio compares the angry, buzzing insect with a shrewish woman.

35

24, 25 *light:* 1) slim, 2) lustful, and 3) lacking a musical accompaniment (cf. the words "burden" in line 23 and "catch" in line 25—both musical terms).
29 *O slow-winged turtle . . . thee:* a "buzzard" was an inferior breed of hawk, able to overtake only the slow-moving turtledove (emblem of faithful love).

Kate starts to exit.

Petruchio, still seated on the chair, stops her with his bawdy pun. He then crosses to her to make peace.

Kate slaps him.

Petruchio grabs her arm, drops his congenial pose, and seriously dares her to strike him again.

A little frightened, Kate tries to release her arm.

Petruchio returns to a playful tone. He is now clearly in charge of this game.

KATHERINA
Yours, if you talk of tails; and so farewell.

PETRUCHIO
What! With my tongue in your tail? Nay, come again,
Good Kate; I am a gentleman—

KATHERINA
                    That I'll try.

PETRUCHIO
I swear I'll cuff you if you strike again.

KATHERINA
So you may lose your arms.
If you strike me, you are no gentleman;
And if no gentleman, why then no arms.

PETRUCHIO
A herald, Kate? O, put me in thy books!

KATHERINA
What is your crest? A coxcomb?

PETRUCHIO
A combless cock, so Kate will be my hen.

KATHERINA
No cock of mine. You crow too like a craven.

PETRUCHIO
Nay, come, Kate, come; you must not look so sour.

KATHERINA
It is my fashion, when I see a crab.

PETRUCHIO
Why, here's no crab, and therefore look not sour.

KATHERINA
There is, there is.

PETRUCHIO
Then show it me.

KATHERINA
                    Had I a glass, I would.

PETRUCHIO
What? You mean my face?

KATHERINA
Well aimed of such a young one.

PETRUCHIO
Now, by Saint George, I am too young for you.

KATHERINA
Yet you are withered.

PETRUCHIO
'Tis with cares.

tails: pun on "tales" or "fairy tales."
40 *come again:* try again.

cuff: slap, strike.

45
arms: coat of arms/bodily limbs.
books: heraldic registers.

crest: family coat of arms/ rooster's "comb." *coxcomb:* cock's crest (also "a cap worn by a court jester or fool"). *combless:* gentle. *craven:* coward (a cock unwilling to fight, signified by its drooping comb). *crab:* crab apple/sour-faced person.

55

glass: mirror.

aimed of: guessed for. *young one:* an ironic insult to the older Petruchio. *Saint George:* the patron saint of England. *too young:* too strong.

Dance music plays again in the background, and Kate starts to leave.

Petruchio takes her arm again and stops her from leaving.

Petruchio has a firm hold on Kate now and makes her dance; he spins her, dips her, and whirls her around so rapidly that by the end of this speech, she has fallen to the floor.

Kate recovers, then walks to the mirror to straighten her clothes and hair.

Petruchio comes up behind her and holds her around the waist. He whispers in her ear.

KATHERINA
I care not.
PETRUCHIO
Nay, hear you, Kate. In sooth, you scape not so.

In sooth: In truth.
scape: escape.

KATHERINA
I chafe you if I tarry. Let me go.

chafe: irritate, annoy. *tarry:*
stay, linger behind. *not a*

PETRUCHIO
No, not a whit. I find you passing gentle.
'Twas told me you were rough and coy and sullen,
And now I find report a very liar;
For thou art pleasant, gamesome, passing courteous,
But slow in speech, yet sweet as spring-time flowers.
Thou canst not frown; thou canst not look askance,
Nor bite the lip, as angry wenches will;
Nor hast thou pleasure to be cross in talk.
But thou with mildness entertain'st thy wooers,
With gentle conference, soft and affable.
Why does the world report that Kate doth limp?
O sland'rous world! Kate like the hazel-twig
Is straight and slender, and as brown in hue
As hazel nuts, and sweeter than the kernels.
O, let me see thee walk. Thou doest not halt.

whit: not in the least. *pass-*
ing: very, exceedingly. *coy:*
disdainful. *very:* complete.

askance: scornfully.

entertain'st: receive.
conference: discussion.
75

halt: limp (cf. line 75).

KATHERINA
Where did you study all this goodly speech?

80

PETRUCHIO
It is extempore, from my mother-wit.

extempore: impromptu,
unstudied. *mother-wit:*
natural intelligence.

KATHERINA
A witty mother! Witless else her son.
PETRUCHIO
Am I not wise?
KATHERINA
Yes, keep you warm.
PETRUCHIO
Marry, so I mean, sweet Katherine, in thy bed.
And therefore, setting all this chat aside,
Thus in plain terms: your father hath consented
That you shall be my wife; your dowry 'greed on;
And, will you, nill you, I will marry you.

85

'greed on: agreed upon.
will you, nill you: whether

75 *limp:* the word may be taken metaphorically (i.e., you walk out of step with other women; you are very different) or literally (through comic stage action Kate is somehow forced to limp) or in both ways.
82 *Witless else her son:* If you had not inherited intelligence from your mother, you would have no wit at all.
84 *keep you warm:* having enough wit "to keep oneself warm" was a well-known proverbial expression.

Baptista enters, sees the two together, and stops. He is carrying two champagne glasses and a bottle, hoping to celebrate a possible engagement. Petruchio kisses Kate passionately. Baptista, assured by this show of affection, speaks to Petruchio.

Kate, embarrassed at being caught kissing Petruchio, crosses away from the men and remains silent.

When she does speak, Kate shouts angrily at her father.

Petruchio and Baptista cross to Kate, each grabbing her by an arm and pulling her offstage. They all argue as they exit.
Portia and Nerissa walk by giggling and break into the end of the *Shrew* scene. They place two chairs close to the mirror, light cigarettes, and begin to gossip conspiratorially. The Male Narrator points toward the two gossiping women.

The Narrators move to a vantage point where they can listen to the conversation between Portia and Nerissa, but not be seen themselves.

Now, Kate, I am a husband for your turn;
For, by this light, whereby I see thy beauty— *you will or not. for your turn: exactly suited for you.*
Thy beauty that doth make me like thee well—
Thou must be married to no man but me.
For I am he am born to tame you, Kate,
And bring you from a wild Kate to a Kate *wild Kate: punning on wildcat.*
Conformable as other household Kates.
Here comes your father. Never make denial:
I must and will have Katherine to my wife.

BAPTISTA
Now, Signior Petruchio, how speed you with my daughter? *how speed you: how successful have you been?*

PETRUCHIO
How but well, sir, how but well? *100*
It were impossible I should speed amiss. *speed amiss: fail.*

BAPTISTA
Why, how now, daughter Katherine? In your dumps? *dumps: bad humor, depression.*

KATHERINA
Call you me daughter? Now, I promise you,
You have showed a tender fatherly regard
To wish me wed to one half lunatic, *105*
A mad-cap ruffian and a swearing Jack, *Jack: rascal.*
That thinks with oaths to face the matter out.

PETRUCHIO
Father, 'tis thus: yourself and all the world
That talked of her have talked amiss of her. *talked amiss of: spoken incorrectly about. policy: cunning motives. froward: unreasonable, ill-humored. hot: violent (of a choleric humour). 'greed: agreed.*
If she be curst, it is for policy:
For she's not froward, but modest as the dove;
She is not hot, but temperate as the morn.
And, to conclude, we have 'greed so well together
That upon Sunday is the wedding day.

KATHERINA
I'll see thee hanged on Sunday first. *115*

MALE NARRATOR
Know you these women?

FEMALE NARRATOR
My lord, I must confess I know these women.

MALE NARRATOR
Away, then; come see the conspirators.

[*The Merchant of Venice,* I.ii]

107 *face the matter out:* boldly pretend (the metaphor is taken from card games, where a face card was often placed on top of a hand to hide weaker cards).

One man appears and stands in the shadows listening to the women.

Another man enters and overhears Portia's comments.

PORTIA

By my troth, Nerissa, my little body is aweary of this great world.

NERISSA

You would be, sweet madam, if your miseries were in the same abundance as your good fortunes are; and yet, for aught I see, they are as sick that surfeit with too much as they that starve with nothing.

surfeit: indulge excessively.

PORTIA

But this reasoning is not in the fashion to choose me a husband. O me, the word "choose"! I may neither choose who I would, nor refuse who I dislike: so is the will of a living daughter curbed by the will of a dead father. Is it not hard, Nerissa, that I cannot choose one nor refuse none?

will . . . will: desire . . . last will and testament.

NERISSA

Your father was ever virtuous. But what warmth is there in your affection towards any of these princely suitors that are already come?

PORTIA

I pray thee, over-name them; and as thou namest them, I will describe them; and, according to my description, level at my affection.

over-name them: recite the list of their names. *level:* guess.

NERISSA

First, there is the Neapolitan prince.

PORTIA

Ay, that's a colt indeed, for he doth nothing but talk of his horse; and he makes it a great appropriation to his own good parts that he can shoe him himself. I am much afeard my lady his mother played false with a smith.

NERISSA

Then there is the County Palatine.

PORTIA

He doth nothing but frown, as who should say, "And you will not have me, choose." He hears merry tales and smiles not; I fear he will prove the weeping philosopher when he grows old, being so full of unmannerly sadness in his youth. I had rather be married to a death's head with a bone in his mouth than to either of these. God defend me from these two!

colt: trick, cheat (with a pun on "young horse"). *appropriation:* addition. *good parts:* reputation. *played false with:* made love with. *smith:* blacksmith (thereby explaining the prince's interest in horses). *County:* Count. *who:* one who. *And:* If. *choose:* do what you like (i.e., choose someone else). *death's-head:* a human skull.

NERISSA

How say you by the French lord, Monsieur Le Bon?

7 *But . . . husband:* But none of this idle chatter will help me choose a husband.

A third man enters into the shadows and overhears the women slander him.

A fourth man and a boy enter to eavesdrop on the women.

Portia looks very satisfied with herself for having disposed of all her suitors.

Then Nerissa surprises her with the news that a new suitor will arrive that evening.

The two women start to exit, then see the four men standing in the shadows. The women laugh and run back into the dance. The men who have been watching Portia and Nerissa are angry and embarrassed; they have been wounded by the women's open scorn for them.

PORTIA

God made him, and therefore let him pass for a man. In truth, I know it is a sin to be a mocker, but *he*, why, he hath a horse better than the Neapolitan's, a better bad habit of frowning than the County Palatine; he is every man in no man. If I should marry him, I should marry twenty husbands. If he would despise me, I would forgive him; for if he love me to madness, I shall never requite him.

I should marry twenty husbands: i.e., he is so changeable. *requite:* return his love.

NERISSA

What say you, then, to Falconbridge, the young baron of England?

PORTIA

You know I say nothing to him, for he understands not me, nor I him. He hath neither Latin, French, nor Italian, and you will come into the court and swear that I have a poor pennyworth in the English. he is a proper man's picture; but, alas, who can converse with a dumb show?

hath: knows, speaks. *a poor pennyworth:* meager ability (in speaking English). *proper man's picture:* very handsome. *a dumb show:* a play without words.

NERISSA

How like you the young German, the Duke of Saxony's nephew?

PORTIA

Very vilely in the morning, when he is sober, and most vilely in the afternoon, when he is drunk. When he is best, he is a little worse than a man; and when he is worst, he is little better than a beast. And the worst fall that ever fell, I hope I shall make shift to go without him.

make shift: manage. *to go without him:* to avoid marrying him. *the having:* i.e., having to marry. *suit:* proposals of marriage.

NERISSA

You need not fear, lady, the having any of these lords. They have acquainted me with their determinations, which is indeed to return to their home and to trouble you with no more suit.

PORTIA

I am glad this parcel of wooers are so reasonable, for there is not one among them but I dote on his very absence, and I pray God grant them a fair departure.

parcel: group.

55

NERISSA

The Prince of Morocco will be here tonight.

PORTIA

If he have the condition of a saint and the complexion of a devil, I had rather he should shrive me than wive me. Come, Nerissa. Whiles we shut the gate upon one wooer, another knocks at the door.

condition: disposition. *complexion of a devil:* i.e., dark (with, perhaps, a pun on his "evil tempera-

---

49 *And the worst fall that ever fell:* If the worst possible thing happens (and he chooses the correct casket).

The Male Narrator goes to the group of four men and a boy and attempts to cheer them up. He then turns back to the Female Narrator.

The group of males stand together and confer noisily on an important matter. They seem to be devising a way to get back at all of these women for ruining their evening. Soon, they urge the boy (Viola/Cesario) to go on an errand for them.
The boy is unwilling to go forward. Finally, one of the men pushes him toward the Female Narrator.

The Female Narrator looks scornfully at the young boy.

Duke Orsino takes hold of Viola and dismisses the other men. All the rest move upstage into the shadows, leaving Orsino and Viola alone together down center.

Orsino retreats to the group of men upstage while urging Viola to go meet Olivia and Maria, who have just entered down right. Viola stands still, too afraid to go forward to meet the women. One of the men in the group, Malvolio, whispers assurance to "him." Malvolio then speaks to Olivia. As they talk, Viola tries to hide behind Malvolio, but "he" is urged forward by all the other men.

FIRST MALE
O, most delicate fiend! Who is't can read a woman?

MALE NARRATOR
You are a thousand times a properer man than she a woman. I know the devil himself will not eat a woman.

FEMALE NARRATOR
Who taught you this?

MALE NARRATOR
I learned it out of women's faces. I charge thee, tell this head-strong woman.

VIOLA/CESARIO
I am unworthy for her schoolmaster.

FIRST MALE
Go to, away!

FEMALE NARRATOR
By my troth, your town is troubled with unruly boys.

ORSINO
Stand you a while aloof.
Thou knowest no less but all. I have unclasped
To thee the book even of my secret soul.
Therefore, good youth, address thy gait unto her;
Be not denied access; stand at her doors,
And tell them there thy fixed foot shall grow
Till thou have audience.

VIOLA
Say I do speak with her, my lord. What then?

ORSINO
O, then unfold the passion of my love;
Surprise her with discourse of my dear faith.
It shall become thee well to act my woes.

VIOLA
I'll do my best to woo your lady.

[*Twelfth Night*, I.v]

MALVOLIO
Madam, yond young fellow swears he will speak with you. I told him you were sick; he takes on him to understand so much, and therefore comes to speak with you. I told him you were asleep; he seems to have a foreknowledge of that too, and

ment"). *shrive me:* hear my confession (like a priest). *read:* understand.

for her schoolmaster: to teach her anything.

70

aloof: apart. *unclasped:* opened (i.e., told you my innermost secrets). *address . . . her:* go to her. *grow:* stay.

unfold: recite. *Surprise her:* Take her suddenly (as in a military attack).

yond: yonder. *takes on him to understand so much:* i.e., says he knows you are sick.

81 *It shall become thee well:* You will look good/you will profit by the action.

Malvolio runs back to the group of men in the shadows. Olivia and Maria place veils over their faces and look at themselves in the mirror.

Viola, finally summoning forth all her courage, steps toward the women.

Viola is nervous that her disguise will be discovered, yet she is also resentful about the rude treatment she is receiving at the hands of Olivia and Maria.

therefore comes to speak with you. What is to be said to him, lady? He's fortified against any denial.

OLIVIA
Tell him he shall not speak with me.

MALVOLIO
'Has been told so; and he says he'll stand at your door like a sheriff's post, and be the supporter to a bench, but he'll speak with you.

OLIVIA
What kind of man is he?

MALVOLIO
Why, of mankind.

OLIVIA
What manner of man?

MALVOLIO
Of very ill manner. He'll speak with you, will you or no.

OLIVIA
Of what personage and years is he?

MALVOLIO
Not yet old enough for a man, nor young enough for a boy. He is very well-favored, and he speaks very shrewishly. One would think his mother's milk were scarce out of him.

OLIVIA
Let him approach. Give me my veil. We'll once more hear Orsino's embassy.

VIOLA
The honorable lady of the house, which is she?

OLIVIA
Speak to me; I shall answer for her. Your will?

VIOLA
Most radiant, exquisite, and unmatchable beauty—I pray you, tell me if this be the lady of the house, for I never saw her. I would be loath to cast away my speech; for besides that it is excellently well penned, I have taken great pains to con it. Good beauties, let me sustain no scorn. I am very comptible, even to the least sinister usage.

OLIVIA
Whence came you, sir?

VIOLA
I can say little more than I have studied, and that question's out

---

5
He's fortified against any denial: i.e., He won't take "no" for an answer.

'Has: He has. *a sheriff's post:* a post upon which official proclamations were placed.

will you or no: whether you will let him or not.
15

well-favored: handsome. *shrewishly:* cleverly, sharply.

embassy: formal declaration of love.

cast away: waste (i.e., deliver it to someone other than Olivia). *con:* memorize. *comptible:* sensitive. *least sinister usage:* slightest discourteous treatment.

out of my part: not part of

---

9 *be the supporter to a bench:* i.e., he is willing to stand next to the bench for so long he will appear to support it.

Maria crosses to Viola and pulls her by the arm toward the exit.

Viola finally loses her temper and snaps at Olivia and Maria.

Olivia, who is both insulted and intrigued by Viola's rude manner, confronts her.

Viola restrains herself a bit, realizing that she must hold her temper for Orsino's sake.

of my part. Good gentle one, give me modest assurance, if you be the lady of the house, that I may proceed in my speech.

OLIVIA
Are you a comedian?

VIOLA
No, my profound heart. And yet, by the very fangs of malice, I swear I am not that I play. Are you the lady of the house?

OLIVIA
If I do not usurp myself, I am.

VIOLA
Most certain, if you are she, you do usurp yourself: for what is yours to bestow is not yours to reserve. But this is from my commission. I will on with my speech in your praise, and then show you the heart of my message.

OLIVIA
Come to what is important in it. I forgive you the praise.

VIOLA
Alas, I took great pains to study it, and 'tis poetical.

OLIVIA
It is the more likely to be feigned; I pray you, keep it in. If you be mad, be gone; if you have reason, be brief. 'Tis not that time of moon with me to make one in so skipping a dialogue.

MARIA
Will you hoist sail, sir? Here lies your way.

VIOLA
No, good swabber; I am here to hull a little longer. Some mollification for your giant, sweet lady!

OLIVIA
What are you? What would you?

VIOLA
The rudeness that hath appeared in me have I learned from my entertainment. What I am and what I would are as secret as maidenhead: to your ears, divinity; to any other's, profanation.

the lines I have memorized.

comedian: actor (a mild insult in this context).
my profound heart: deeply beloved.

do not usurp myself: am not an imposter.

from my commission: outside of my duties.
heart: center of meaning/ Orsino's "heart."
forgive you: excuse you from reciting.

keep it in: do not deliver it to me.
make one: take part. *skipping:* frivolous.

hull: a nautical term meaning "to stay in port with sails furled." *Some mollification:* Please control.

50
entertainment: rude reception at the gate. *maiden-*

34 *by the very fangs of malice:* "malice" is metaphorically depicted as a poisonous snake (perhaps in response to Olivia's comic insult in line 33).

37 *you do usurp yourself:* by rejecting Orsino's proposal, you are not behaving as Olivia should; therefore, you usurp yourself.

44–45 *'Tis not that time of moon with me:* lunacy (madness) was thought to be effected by the changing phases of the moon. This may also be a reference to Olivia's menstrual cycle.

47 *swabber:* a sailor who performs such menial duties as washing the deck of a ship (a derogatory response to Maria's "Will you hoist sail, sir?").

48 *giant:* an ironic reference, no doubt, to the tiny Maria. In Arthurian romances, giants often guarded captive ladies.

Olivia is convinced that Viola will behave properly, so she asks Maria to leave. Maria exits down right.

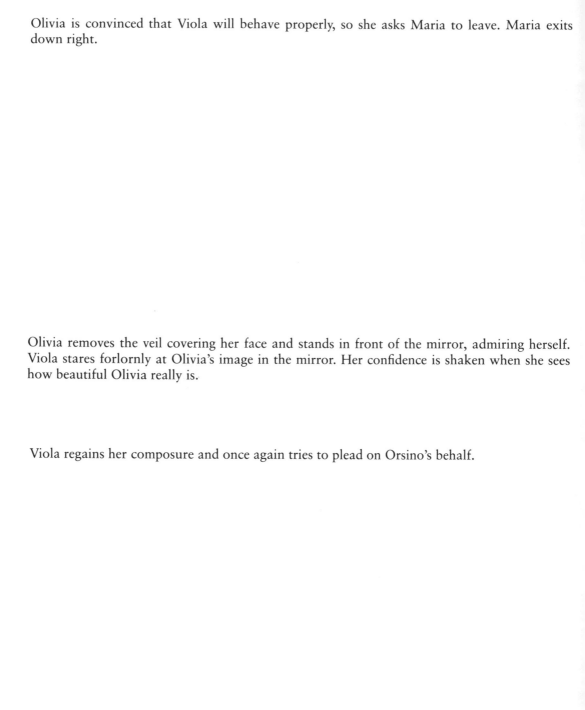

Olivia removes the veil covering her face and stands in front of the mirror, admiring herself. Viola stares forlornly at Olivia's image in the mirror. Her confidence is shaken when she sees how beautiful Olivia really is.

Viola regains her composure and once again tries to plead on Orsino's behalf.

OLIVIA
Give us the place alone; we will hear this divinity. Now, sir, what
is your text?

VIOLA
Most sweet lady—

OLIVIA
A comfortable doctrine, and much may be said of it. Where lies
your text?

VIOLA
In Orsino's bosom.

OLIVIA
In his bosom? In what chapter of his bosom?

VIOLA
To answer by the method, in the first of his heart.

OLIVIA
O, I have read it; it is heresy. Have you no more to say?

VIOLA
Good madam, let me see your face.

OLIVIA
Have you any commission from your lord to negotiate with my
face? You are now out of your text. But we will draw the curtain
and show you the picture. Look you, sir; such a one I was this
present. Is't not well done?

VIOLA
Excellently done, if God did all.

OLIVIA
'Tis in grain, sir; 'twill endure wind and weather.

VIOLA
'Tis beauty truly blent, whose red and white
Nature's own sweet and cunning hand laid on.
Lady, you are the cruellest she alive
If you will lead these graces to the grave
And leave the world no copy.

OLIVIA
O, sir, I will not be so hard-hearted. I will give out divers schedules of my beauty. It shall be inventoried and every particle and
utensil labelled to my will: as, *item*, two lips, indifferent red;
item, two grey eyes, with lids to them; *item*, one neck; one chin;
and so forth. Were you sent hither to praise me?

head: virginity.

55

comfortable: comforting.

first: the first chapter.

commission: permission.
out of: departing from.
curtain: veil. *this present:*
i.e., the "painting" has just
been completed.

in grain: i.e., the paint is
dry on the canvas and
won't wash off. *blent:*
blended. *cunning:* skillful.
laid on: painted.

divers schedules: various
lists.
utensil: item. *labelled:*
appended, added as a
codicil to a will.

---

60 *To answer by the method:* To continue this metaphor, through which Orsino's message is compared to the text of
a sermon (cf. "divinity," "doctrine," and "heresy").
72–73 *lead . . . copy:* die without bearing a child (who would be a living "copy" of your beauty).

Viola sets aside her memorized speeches and talks sincerely to Olivia.

Though her plea is addressed to Olivia, Viola is undoubtedly describing her own love for Orsino in these lines.

Olivia is impressed. She is clearly becoming enamored with this young man.

VIOLA
I see you what you are: you are too proud.
But if you were the devil, you are fair.
My lord and master loves you: O, such love
Could be but recompensed, though you were crowned
The nonpareil of beauty!

OLIVIA
                         How does he love me?

VIOLA
With adorations, fertile tears,
With groans that thunder love, with sighs of fire.

OLIVIA
Your lord does know my mind: I cannot love him.
Yet I suppose him virtuous, know him noble,
Of great estate, of fresh and stainless youth;
In voices well divulg'd, free, learn'd, and valiant;
And in dimension and the shape of nature,
A gracious person. But yet I cannot love him:
He might have took his answer long ago.

VIOLA
If I did love you in my master's flame,
With such a suff'ring, such a deadly life,
In your denial I would find no sense;
I would not understand it.

OLIVIA
                         Why, what would you?

VIOLA
Make me a willow cabin at your gate
And call upon my soul within the house;
Write loyal cantons of contemned love
And sing them loud even in the dead of night;
Hallow your name to the reverberate hills
And make the babbling gossip of the air
Cry out "Olivia!" O, you should not rest
Between the elements of air and earth
But you should pity me!

OLIVIA
                         You might do much.
What is your parentage?

if: even if.

nonpareil: one who has no equal.

85

Of great estate: Wealthy. *stainless:* free from moral blemish. *In voices well divulg'd:* Held high in public opinion. *dimension . . . nature:* form and physique. *in:* with. *flame:* passionate intensity. *deadly:* morbid, melancholy.

what would you?: what would *you* do? *willow cabin:* the willow was a conventional symbol of unrequited love. *my soul:* Olivia. *cantons:* songs. *contemned:* unrequited, rejected. *Hallow:* Sing out/Make holy. *reverberate:* resounding. *babbling gossip of the air:* echo. *Between . . . earth:* Anywhere on earth.

81–83 *O . . . beauty:* Orsino loves you so much that even if you were the most beautiful woman imaginable, you could barely repay his devotion to you.

85 *fertile:* abundant (the implication is that Orsino cries enough to make the earth fertile).

Sensing Olivia's interest in her, Viola reaffirms the mask of the "boy," lowers her voice, and assumes a manly pose.

Olivia attempts to hand Viola money. Viola refuses the offer and storms back to the group of men.

The Narrators watch the "boy" depart. The Male Narrator has been outraged by all the women he has encountered this evening. The other men join him as he turns to a new woman, Hermione, who has entered and is standing alone. He speaks to her in the following sonnet.

Hermione is brought into the circle of men. The Male Narrator addresses everyone on the stage and in the audience.

VIOLA   110
Above my fortunes, yet my state is well:
I am a gentleman.
OLIVIA
                    Get you to your lord.
I cannot love him; let him send no more—
Unless, perchance, you come to me again   *it:* my refusal.
To tell me how he takes it. Fare you well.
I thank you for your pains. Spend this for me.
VIOLA
I am no fee'd post, lady; keep your purse.   *fee'd post:* common mes-
My master, not myself, lacks recompense.   senger who accepts tips.
Love make his heart of flint that you shall love,
And let your fervor, like my master's, be   *fervor:* passion.
Placed in contempt! Farewell, fair cruelty.   *cruelty:* cruel person.

[*Sonnet 61*]

MALE NARRATOR
To be thus taunted, scorned, and baited at!   *baited at:* tormented.
Is it thy will thy image should keep open   *will:* desire. *image:* mem-
My heavy eyelids to the weary night?   ory.
Dost thou desire my slumbers should be broken,   *broken:* disturbed.
While shadows like to thee do mock my sight?   5
Is it thy spirit that thou send'st from thee
So far from home into my deeds to pry,
To find out shames and idle hours in me,
The scope and tenure of thy jealousy?   *scope . . . jealousy:* range
O no, thy love, though much, is not so great;   and persistence of your
It is my love that keeps mine eye awake,   suspicion.
Mine own true love that doth my rest defeat,
To play the watchman ever for thy sake.
        For thee watch I, whilst thou dost wake elsewhere, *watch:* remain awake.
        From me far off, with others all too near.   *wake:* revel, have a good
FIRST MALE   time.
Damn her, lewd minx! O, damn her!   *minx:* a wanton woman.
SECOND MALE
See the hell of having a false woman!
MALE NARRATOR
This woman's an easy glove, my lord: she goes off and on at

---

119 *Love make his heart of flint:* i.e., I hope that Love turns the heart of any man you adore to the hardest flint.

The Male Narrator, who has now become Leontes, steps forward and prepares to accuse Hermione, who is the defendant in this trial. Three men sit in chairs facing upstage and stare at Hermione. The officer reads the indictment, then stands off to the left. The Female Narrator is stage right, near the group of men. The men have now become part of the audience, and Hermione appeals to them and to the audience as if to a jury.

Hermione alternates her appeal to the entire court, then to Leontes alone.

pleasure. Look upon her. Do you see, gentlemen? Nay, guiltiness
will speak.   20

[*The Winter's Tale,* III.ii]

LEONTES
Read the indictment.

OFFICER
"Hermione, Queen to the worthy Leontes, King of Sicilia, thou
art here accused and arraigned of high treason, in committing
adultery with Polixenes, King of Bohemia, and conspiring with
Camillo to take away the life of our soverign lord the King, thy
royal husband: the pretense whereof being by circumstances
partly laid open, thou, Hermione, contrary to the faith and al-
legiance of a true subject, didst counsel and aid them, for their
better safety, to fly away by night."

Camillo: an honest, trusted
counselor to King Leontes.
pretense: purpose, design.
them: Polixenes and Camillo. *to fly away:* to escape.

HERMIONE
Since what I am to say must be but that
Which contradicts my accusation, and
The testimony on my part no other
But what comes from myself, it shall scarce boot me
To say "not guilty." Mine integrity,
Being counted falsehood, shall, as I express it,
Be so received. But thus, if powers divine
Behold our human actions (as they do),
I doubt not then but innocence shall make
False accusation blush, and tyranny
Tremble at patience. You, my lord, best know
(Who least will seem to do so) my past life
Hath been as continent, as chaste, as true,
As I am now unhappy; which is more
Than history can pattern, though devised
And played to take spectators. For behold me—
A fellow of the royal bed, which owe
A moiety of the throne, a great king's daughter,
The mother to a hopeful prince—here standing
To prate and talk for life and honor 'fore
Who please to come and hear. For life, I prize it
As I weigh grief, which I would spare; for honor,

10

no other: i.e., no one else
will speak in my behalf.
boot: profit, help.
it: my defense to these
charges (my "integrity").
so: as a lie.

at: in the face of. *You, my
lord:* delivered to Leontes,
her husband. *to do so:* i.e.,
to recognize Hermione's
honorable behavior. *continent:* self-restrained.
which: which unhappiness.
history: story, fiction. *pattern:* provide a similar
example for. *take:* attract,
please. *fellow:* partner.
which owe: who owns.

30–33 *For life . . . stand for:* I value life as I do grief, and I could easily give both up; but honor, which descends
from me to my children, is important enough to fight for.

One of the men leans toward the Female Narrator and whispers to her.

'Tis a derivative from me to mine,
And only that I stand for. I appeal
To your own conscience, sir, before Polixenes
Came to your court, how I was in your grace,
How merited to be so; since he came,
With what encounter so uncurrent I
Have strained t'appear thus; if one jot beyond
The bound of honor, or in act or will
That way inclining, hardened be the hearts
Of all that hear me, and my near'st of kin
Cry "fie" upon my grave! For Polixenes,
With whom I am accused, I do confess
I loved him as in honor he required;
With such a kind of love as might become
A lady like me; with a love even such,
So, and no other, as yourself commanded.
SECOND MALE
The lady doth protest too much, methinks.
FEMALE NARRATOR
O, but she'll keep her word.
HERMIONE
                    Now, for conspiracy,
I know not how it tastes, though it be dished
For me to try how. All I know of it
Is that Camillo was an honest man—
And why he left your court, the gods themselves,
Wotting no more than I, are ignorant.
LEONTES
You knew of his departure, as you know
What you have underta'en to do in's absence.
HERMIONE
Sir,
You speak a language that I understand not;
My life stands in the level of your dreams,
which I'll lay down.

moiety: share. hopeful: one in whom we place our hopes. prate: talk wildly. 'fore: before. Who please: Whoever wishes.

jot: particle. or . . . or: either . . . or. will: desire.

required: deserved. 45 such: of this kind.

50

Wotting: Knowing.

underta'en: undertaken, attempted. in's: in his.

level: aim. dreams: fantasy. 60

36 How merited to be so: What I had done to deserve your favor.
36–38 since he came . . . t'appear thus: since Polixenes' arrival, what unlawful or immoral deed have I committed to be thus on trial?
50–52 Now . . . how: Even if I were served a dish of conspiracy, I would not recognize its taste.
59–60 My life . . . down: You suspect my faithfulness because of your own lewd dreams, which I'll challenge and dispute.

Leontes rises from his chair and confronts Hermione. He can no longer contain his anger, and he attacks her verbally, appealing all the while to the other men onstage.

Hermione realizes the hopelessness of her situation: that no amount of pleading will sway Leontes or the all-male jury. Yet she courageously continues, speaking firmly and deeply from her innermost soul.

LEONTES

                Your actions are my dreams.
You had a bastard by Polixenes,
And I but dreamed it! As you were past all shame
(Those of your fact are so), so past all truth,
Which to deny concerns more than avails; for as
Thy brat hath been cast out, like to itself,
No father owning it (which is, indeed,
More criminal in thee than it), so thou
Shalt feel our justice, in whose easiest passage
Look for no less than death.

HERMIONE

                    Sir, spare your threats.
The bug which you would fright me with, I seek.
To me can life be no commodity:
The crown and comfort of my life—your favor—
I do give lost, for I do feel it gone,
But know not how it went; my second joy
And first-fruits of my body, from his presence
I am barred, like one infectious; my third comfort,
Starred most unluckily, is from my breast,
The innocent milk in it most innocent mouth,
Haled out to murder; myself on every post
Proclaimed a strumpet, with immodest hatred
The child-bed privilege denied, which 'longs
To women of all fashion; lastly, hurried
Here to this place, i' th'open air, before
I have got strength of limit. Now, my liege,
Tell me what blessings I have here alive,
That I should fear to die? Therefore, proceed.
But yet hear this; mistake me not. No life,
I prize it not a straw. But for mine honor,
Which I would free—if I shall be condemned
Upon surmises, all proofs sleeping else
But what your jealousies awake—I tell you
'Tis rigor and not law. Your honors all,

65

brat: illegitimate child. *like to itself*: as it was born. *owning*: claiming responsibility for. *More . . . it*: Your guilt is greater than your child's. *easiest passage*: most lenient sentence. *no less than death*: i.e., I may impose torture, too. *bug*: bugbear, "bogey man" (i.e., death). *commodity*: asset. *give*: consider. *my second joy*: my first child (Mamillius). *my third comfort*: my second child (Perdita). *Starred most unluckily*: Ill-fated. *from*: taken from. *it*: its. *Haled out to*: Dragged forward and accused of. *post*: a wooden stake where public notices were "posted." *immodest*: intemperate, cruel. *'longs*: belongs. *all fashion*: every rank and social position. *got strength of limit*: regained my strength following childbirth. *That*: So that. *No life*: I do not beg

61 *Your actions are my dreams:* Your infidelity has fulfilled my own worst nightmares (also, perhaps, my dreams are preoccupied with thoughts of your lascivious behavior).

64 *Those of your fact are so:* As are all those who have done what you did.

65 *Which . . . avails:* i.e., your denials, which are not surprising under the circumstances, are not worth making.

92–93 *all . . . awake:* i.e., you only listen to (awaken) evidence which you wish to hear.

Three spotlights are focused on Hermione, the Male Narrator, and the Female Narrator. The spotlights on Hermione and the Female Narrator dim to low level, while the spot on the Male Narrator remains bright. After the Male Narrator's last line, the stage goes black.

Black out.

I do refer me to the oracle:
Apollo be my judge!
MALE NARRATOR
Frailty, thy name is woman.

for life. *I prize it not a straw:* My life is worth less to me than a straw. *free:* clear of the slander now attached to it. *surmises:* unfounded conjectures. *rigor:* harsh tyranny. *refer me:* ask to be judged by. *the oracle:* Apollo's shrine at Delphi.

The time is much later that same night at the party. The chairs are left onstage as they were at the end of act I. The Male Narrator stumbles on stage groggy, exhausted, and perhaps a bit hung over. His tie is untied, and his tuxedo has a rumpled, slept-in look. He tries to clear his head and straighten himself out in front of the mirrors.

From darkened corners of the stage, from all directions, he hears women's voices. At first, the voices seem to be coming from inside his head, as if they were part of some terrible nightmare. Percussive musical sounds accompany the words.

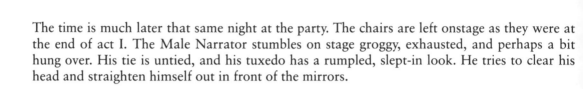

From upstage, the Female Narrator enters and walks toward the Male Narrator, speaking directly to him.

The women's voices begin to call out this litany of words, first whispering, then overlapping and echoing each other. The percussion sounds continue to underscore the words.

Act II
Her Infinite Variety

MALE NARRATOR
'Tis now the very witching time of night,   *witching:* bewitching.
When churchyards yawn and hell itself breathes out
Contagion to this world. Now could I drink hot blood   *Contagion:* Evil spirits.
And do such bitter business as the day
Would quake to look on.   *quake:* tremble.
FIRST FEMALE
Who can accuse me?
SECOND FEMALE
Let them accuse me by invention.
THIRD FEMALE
They cannot praise us, as little accuse us.
FOURTH FEMALE
It is no fault of mine.
ALL FEMALES
The fault is thine!   10
MALE NARRATOR
Welcome, ladies, welcome.
FIRST FEMALE
Women may fall when there is no strength in men.
FEMALE NARRATOR
Now is my turn to speak,
To unmask falsehood and bring truth to light.
Women! Shakespeare's Women!   15
ALL FEMALES
        Gallant
        Powerful

The words and percussion sounds continue toward a crescendo, then stop abruptly. The Female Narrator speaks clearly to the audience.
The Male Narrator sits in one of the chairs, facing upstage, and is now ready to hear the Female Narrator's presentation.

Rosalind, dressed like a boy in a tuxedo, crosses the stage and stops up center. She is feeling alone and out of place. Orlando, who is tired and lonely and looking for someone to talk to, goes up to the boy and speaks to him.

Orlando passes his champagne bottle to Rosalind, who takes a swig.

Mournful
Desperate
Lonely   20
Lovely
Loving
Beloved
Sad
Steadfast   25
Fancy-free
Merciful
Passionate
Mirthful
False   30
Loyal
True
Conquered
Victorious

FEMALE NARRATOR
Age cannot wither nor custom stale her infinite variety. *stale:* make stalc.
MALE NARRATOR
Sweet madam, I am ready now.
Lead in your ladies, everyone.

[*As You Like It,* III.ii]

ORLANDO
Are you native of this place?

ROSALIND
As the cony that you see dwell where she is kindled. *cony:* rabbit. *kindled:* born.

ORLANDO
Your accent is something finer than you could purchase in so removed a dwelling. *purchase:* learn, acquire. *so removed:* so far from civilization.

ROSALIND
I have been told so of many. But indeed an old religious uncle of mine taught me to speak, who was in his youth an inland man—one that knew courtship too well, for there he fell in love. I have heard him read many lectures against it; and I thank God I am not a woman, to be touched with so many giddy offenses as he hath generally taxed their whole sex withal.

religious: member of a religious order. *inland:* i.e., from a city.

touched: tainted, afflicted. *taxed:* charged. *generally:* universally.

ORLANDO
Can you remember any of the principal evils that he laid to the charge of women?

laid to the charge of women: charged women with.

Feeling very chummy, Rosalind takes out a linen party napkin and shares some cake from the party with Orlando. They sit on the floor and drink and eat while they talk.

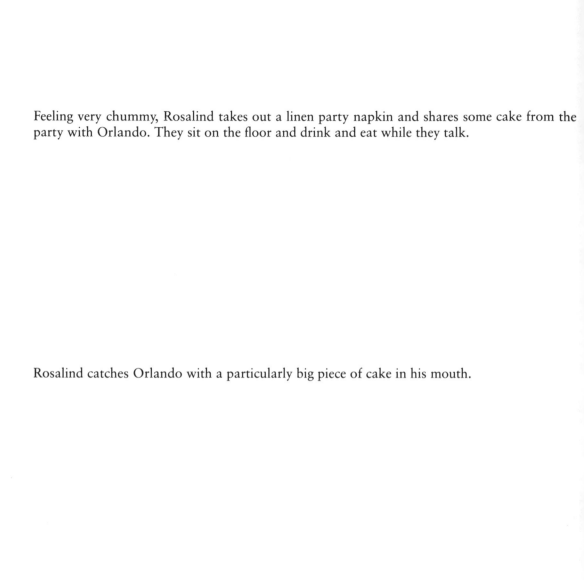

Rosalind catches Orlando with a particularly big piece of cake in his mouth.

ROSALIND
There were none principal. They were all like one another as halfpence are: every one fault seeming monstrous till his fellow-fault came to match it.

ORLANDO
I prithee, recount some of them.

recount: list.

ROSALIND
No. I will not cast away my physic but on those that are sick. There is a man haunts the forest that abuses our young plants with carving "Rosalind" on their barks, hangs odes upon hawthorns, and elegies on brambles—all, forsooth, deifying the name of Rosalind. If I could meet that fancy-monger, I would give him some good counsel, for he seems to have the quotidian of love upon him.

physic: medicine.
plants: trees and shrubs.

fancy-monger: someone who deals in (sells) love. *quotidian:* a recurring fever (i.e., love-sick). *love-shaked;* shaken by chills and fever (cf. line 22 above). *marks:* outward

ORLANDO
I am he that is so love-shaked. I pray you, tell me your remedy.

ROSALIND
There is none of my uncle's marks upon you. He taught me how to know a man in love, in which cage of rushes I am sure you are not prisoner.

symptoms. *cage of rushes:* i.e., a flimsy prison (perhaps with a reference to Moses).

ORLANDO
What were his marks?

blue eye: dark circles under the eyes (caused by weeping). *unquestionable spirit:* compulsion to shun conversation (unwilling to be questioned). *bonnet unbanded:* a hat without a band around its crown. *careless:* neglectful of one's appearance. *point-device:* exactly correct.

ROSALIND
A lean cheek, which you have not; a blue eye and sunken, which you have not; an unquestionable spirit, which you have not; a beard neglected, which you have not—but I pardon you for that, for simply your having in beard is a younger brother's revenue. Then your hose should be ungartered, your bonnet unbanded, your sleeve unbuttoned, your shoe untied, and everything about you demonstrating a careless desolation. But you are no such man; you are rather point-device in your accoutrements, as loving yourself, than seeming the lover of any other.

ORLANDO
Fair youth, I would I could make thee believe I love.

ROSALIND
Me believe it? You may as soon make her that you love believe it, which I warrant she is apter to do than to confess she does.

apter: more willing.

32 *simply . . . revenue:* speaking frankly, your sparse beard is excusable, since you are still a young man (with the additional sense that younger brothers traditionally received small inheritances).

36–37 *as loving . . . other:* your close attention to such personal details suggests that you love yourself more than you love any woman.

Rosalind, feeling very comfortable and brave at this point with Orlando, lounges back on the ground, hands behind her head.

Orlando is transfixed by the boy's wisdom.

That is one of the points in the which women still give the lie to their consciences. But in good sooth, are you he that hangs the verses on the trees, wherein Rosalind is so admired?

ORLANDO

I swear to thee, youth, by the white hand of Rosalind, I am that he, that unfortunate he.

45

ROSALIND

But are you so much in love as your rhymes speak?

ORLANDO

Neither rhyme nor reason can express how much.

ROSALIND

Love is merely a madness, and, I tell you, deserves as well a dark house and a whip as madmen do; and the reason why they are not so punished and cured is that the lunacy is so ordinary that the whippers are in love too. Yet I profess curing it by counsel.

ORLANDO

Did you ever cure any so?

ROSALIND

Yes, one—and in this manner. He was to imagine me his love, his mistress; and I set him every day to woo me. At which time would I, being but a moonish youth, grieve, be effeminate, changeable, longing and liking, proud, fantastical, apish, shallow, inconstant, full of tears, full of smiles. For every passion something, and for no passion truly anything, as boys and women are for the most part cattle of this color: would now like him, now loathe him; then entertain him, then forswear him; now weep for him, then spit at him; that I drave my suitor from his mad humor of love to a living humor of madness, which was, to forswear the full stream of the world and to live in a nook merely monastic. And thus I cured him. And this way will I take upon me to wash your liver as clean as a sound sheep's heart, that there shall not be one spot of love in't.

ORLANDO

I would not be cured, youth.

ROSALIND

I would cure you, if you would but call me "Rosalind" and come every day to my cote and woo me.

good sooth: plain, honest truth.

merely: completely. *deserves . . . as madmen do:* a common treatment of the insane. *ordinary:* common. *profess:* claim skill in.

set: commanded (as a task). *moonish:* changeable (like the moon). *apish:* affected.

cattle of this color: beasts who behave in this same way. *drave:* drove. *mad humor:* love melancholy. *merely:* completely. *monastic:* like a monk or hermit. *liver:* the supposed bodily source of the passions, especially of love. *sound:* healthy.

cote: cottage.

41–42 *still give the lie to their consciences:* continually run counter to their inner thoughts.

57–58 *For every passion . . . anything:* i.e., She would display every type of passion, though she would truly feel none of them.

61–62 *from his mad humor . . . madness:* from his fashionable love melancholy to a real madness.

67 *I would not be cured, youth:* i.e., I am so sick with love that you will be unable to cure me.

As Orlando and Rosalind are exiting, the Female Narrator pulls off Rosalind's cap, and her long hair comes tumbling out. The other women enter from different parts of the stage, cheering at Rosalind's victory, and then they all sit together on the upstage platforms.

From the group of women onstage, Helena rushes forward, apparently looking for her husband, Bertram. She is nervous, worried, and exhausted, but tries to keep her wits about her. Parolles, Bertram's friend, enters and begins flirting with her.

Parolles traps Helena and tries to kiss her. She uses her wit and all her remaining strength to escape from him.

ORLANDO
Now, by the faith of my love, I will. Tell me where it is.   70
ROSALIND
Go with me to it, and I'll show it you; and by the way you shall
tell me where in the forest you live. Will you go?
ORLANDO
With all my heart, good youth.
FEMALE NARRATOR
You have put him down, lady; you have put him down.

[*All's Well That Ends Well,* I.i]

PAROLLES
Save you, fair queen!
HELENA
And you, monarch!
PAROLLES
No.
HELENA
And no.
PAROLLES
Are you meditating on virginity?   5
HELENA
Ay. You have some stain of soldier in you; let me ask you a | *stain:* small amount.
question: Man is enemy to virginity; how may we barricado it | *barricado:* barricade, pro-
against him? | tect.
PAROLLES
Keep him out.
HELENA
But he assails, and our virginity, though valiant, in the defense | *assails:* attacks violently.
yet is weak. Unfold to us some warlike resistance. | *Unfold:* Suggest.
PAROLLES
There is none. Man, setting down before you, will undermine
you and blow you up.
HELENA
Bless our poor virginity from underminers and blowers up! Is
there no military policy how virgins might blow up men? | *policy:* strategy.

1–2 *queen . . . monarch:* each addresses the other by exaggerated titles, which they both deny in lines 3–4.

12–13 *Man . . . blow you up:* Parolles continues the military metaphor by comparing men to an army preparing to lay siege to a town (women's virginity). Bawdy puns are present in "undermine" (conquer sexually) and "blow you up" (impregnate).

While Helena stands there triumphantly, enjoying her victory over Parolles, her husband, Bertram, enters. Parolles scrambles into the shadows so that Bertram will not see him.

Helena, obviously deeply in love with her husband, kneels before him in a devoted posture. Bertram has been avoiding her all night. Now physically sick from too much drinking, he wants to leave Helena as soon as possible to nurse his hangover. Through this scene, Helena tries desperately to overcome his disdain and ill humor.

PAROLLES

Virginity being blown down, man will quicklier be blown up. Marry, in blowing him down again, with the breach yourselves made, you lose your city. It is not politic in the commonwealth of nature to preserve virginity. Loss of virginity is rational increase, and there was never virgin got till virginity was first lost. That you were made of is metal to make virgins. Virginity by being once lost may be ten times found: by being ever kept, it is ever lost. 'Tis too cold a companion. Away with it!

be blown up: achieve an erection. *Marry:* By the Virgin Mary (a common oath). *politic:* wise. *rational increase:* a sensible way to create more human beings. *got:* begotten, born. *That:* That which.

HELENA

I will stand for't a little, though therefore I die a virgin.

stand for't: defend it (with a phallic pun).

25

PAROLLES

Your husband's coming.

FEMALE NARRATOR

Alas, poor lady! 'Tis hard bondage to become the wife of a detesting lord.

[*All's Well That Ends Well*, II.v]

HELENA

I have, sir, as I was commanded from you,
Spoke with the King, and have procured his leave
For present parting; only he desires
Some private speech with you.

from: by.
procured: obtained. *his . . . parting:* his permission to depart. *only he:* he only.

BERTRAM

                    I shall obey his will.

You must not marvel, Helen, at my course,
Which holds not color with the time, nor does
The ministration and required office
On my particular. Prepared I was not
For such a business; therefore am I found
So much unsettled. This drives me to entreat you
That presently you take your way for home;
And rather muse than ask why I entreat you,
For my respects are better than they seem,
And my appointments have in them a need

course: course of action.
holds . . . color: is not appropriate to. *nor does . . . particular:* nor does it suit my new office as husband.
presently: immediately.
take your way: leave.
muse: wonder about my motives. *respects:* reasons,

17–18 *Marry . . . city:* i.e., By satisfying man's lust, the woman will lose her virginity.

21 *metal:* i.e., your proper purpose in life is to produce children (virgins). Parolles puns on metal/mettle (building material/temperament).

22 *ten times found:* i.e., one former virgin may bear ten children (new virgins).

22–23 *by being ever kept, it is ever lost:* when a woman remains a virgin, she forfeits the opportunity to produce future virgins; as a result, potential virginity is "lost."

Bertram pulls out a letter for his mother.

Bertram attempts to brush past her and leave.

She continues to hold him there with her appeals.

Helena shyly but persistently stays with Bertram, seeking a kiss from him.

When he hears her request, he pushes past her and reaches for Parolles, who helps him offstage.

Greater than shows itself at the first view
To you that know them not. This to my mother.
'Twill be two days ere I shall see you, so
I leave you to your wisdom.

HELENA

               Sir, I can nothing say,
But that I am your most obedient servant.

BERTRAM

Come, come; no more of that.

HELENA

                And ever shall
With true observance seek to eke out that
Wherein toward me my homely stars have failed
To equal my great fortune.

BERTRAM

            Let that go.
My haste is very great. Farewell. Hie home.

HELENA

Pray, sir, your pardon.

BERTRAM

         Well, what would you say?

HELENA

I am not worthy of the wealth I owe,
Nor dare I say 'tis mine—and yet it is;
But, like a timorous thief, most fain would steal
What law does vouch mine own.

BERTRAM

           What would you have?

HELENA

Something, and scarce so much—nothing, indeed.
I would not tell you what I would, my lord.
Faith, yes.
Strangers and foes do sunder, and not kiss.

BERTRAM

I pray you, stay not, but in haste to horse.

HELENA

I shall not break your bidding, good my lord.

BERTRAM

Go thou toward home: where I will never come
Whilst I can shake my sword or hear the drum.
Away, and for our flight.

PAROLLES

        Bravely, coragio!

motives. *appointments:*
purposes. *than:* than that
which.

20

observance: duty, service.
eke out: add to.
homely stars: humble birth.

Hie: Hurry.

30

owe: own, possess.

timorous: timid, fearful.
fain: gladly. *vouch:* grant.

35

sunder: part.

stay: delay.

break: disobey.

coragio: courage, well done.

Helena retreats to the women on the platforms.

Another woman, Ophelia, comes forward and stares after Bertram and Parolles. She seems confused and in need of help. She crosses to the Male Narrator (Polonius) and speaks to him. He attempts to calm her down.

FIRST FEMALE
Poor lady, she were better love a dream.   45
SECOND FEMALE
Were I his lady, I would poison that vile rascal.
THIRD FEMALE
He has much worthy blame laid upon him for shaking off so
good a wife.

[*Hamlet,* II.i]

MALE NARRATOR
How now, Ophelia; what's the matter?
OPHELIA
O my lord, my lord; I have been so affrighted!   *affrighted:* frightened.
POLONIUS
With what, in the name of God?
OPHELIA
My lord, as I was sewing in my closet,   *closet:* room.
Lord Hamlet, with his doublet all unbraced,   *unbraced:* unlaced.
No hat upon his head, his stockings fouled,   *fouled:* rumpled.
Ungartered, and down-gyved to his ankle,   *down-gyved:* fallen to his
Pale as his shirt, his knees knocking each other,   ankle (like chains on a
And with a look so piteous in purport   convict). *purport:* effect.
As if he had been loosed out of hell   *loosed:* released.
To speak of horrors, he comes before me.
POLONIUS
Mad for thy love?
OPHELIA
                My lord, I do not know;
But truly I do fear it.
POLONIUS
                What said he?   15
OPHELIA
He took me by the wrist and held me hard;
Then goes he to the length of all his arm,
And, with his other hand thus o'er his brow,
He falls to such perusal of my face   *perusal of:* gazing upon.
As he would draw it. Long stayed he so.   *As:* As if.
At last, a little shaking of mine arm,
And thrice his head thus waving up and down,
He raised a sigh so piteous and profound   *profound:* deep, meaning-
As it did seem to shatter all his bulk   ful. *bulk:* body.

The Female Narrator tries to lead Ophelia away.

Ophelia starts to follow the Female Narrator, but Hamlet enters and speaks to her. He too is disheveled, still a little drunk, and in a state of deep despair.

When Ophelia hears him speak, she stops and turns toward him.

Ophelia removes the material she used as a veil in the *Twelfth Night* scene and hands it to Hamlet. He refuses to take it, and it drops to the ground between them.

And end his being. That done, he lets me go,   25
And, with his head over his shoulder turned,
He seemed to find his way without his eyes,
For out o' doors he went without their helps,   *helps:* help, assistance.
And, to the last, bended their light on me.   *bended their light:* looked.
FEMALE NARRATOR
I hear him coming. Let's withdraw.   30
SECOND FEMALE
He has much worthy blame laid upon him for shaking off so
sweet a lady.

[*Hamlet*, III.i]

HAMLET
       Soft you now,
The fair Ophelia. Nymph, in thy orisons   *orisons:* prayers.
Be all my sins rememb'red.
OPHELIA
       Good my lord,
How does your honor for this many a day?   5
HAMLET
I humbly thank you: well, well, well.
OPHELIA
My lord, I have remembrances of yours   *remembrances:* gifts.
That I have longed long to redeliver.   *longed long:* wanted for a
I pray you now receive them.   long time.
HAMLET
       No, not I;   10
I never gave you aught.   *aught:* any.
OPHELIA
My honored lord, you know right well you did,   *right:* very.
And with them words of so sweet breath composed
As made the things more rich. Their perfume lost,
Take these again, for to the noble mind   15
Rich gifts wax poor when givers prove unkind.   *wax poor:* become worth-
There, my lord.   less (i.e., lose their senti-
HAMLET   mental value).
Ha, ha! Are you honest?   *honest:* truthful/virtuous.
OPHELIA
My lord?
HAMLET
Are you fair?   *fair:* attractive/just.

Hamlet shares this ironic observation with the Male Narrator.

Hamlet walks over to the Male Narrator and stands at his side while motioning for Ophelia to leave the foyer.

Hamlet starts to leave, but when he hears her response, he loses all control and grabs her arm with one hand and the discarded veil with the other. He pulls her to the fourth-wall mirror and roughly begins rubbing the makeup off her face.

OPHELIA
What means your lordship?

HAMLET
That if you be honest and fair, your honesty should admit no discourse to your beauty.

OPHELIA
Could beauty, my lord, have better commerce than with honesty?

HAMLET
Ay, truly. For the power of beauty will sooner transform honesty from what it is to a bawd, than the force of honesty can translate beauty into his likeness. This was sometime a paradox, but now the time gives it proof. I did love you once.

OPHELIA
Indeed, my lord, you made me believe so.

HAMLET
You should not have believed me, for virtue cannot so inoculate our old stock but we shall relish of it. I loved you not.

OPHELIA
I was the more deceived.

HAMLET
Get thee to a nunnery. Why wouldst thou be a breeder of sinners? I am myself indifferent honest, but yet I could accuse me of such things that it were better my mother had not borne me: I am very proud, revengeful, ambitious, with more offenses at my beck than I have thoughts to put them in, imagination to give them shape, or time to act them in. What should such fellows as I do, crawling between earth and heaven? We are arrant knaves all; believe none of us. Go thy ways to a nunnery. Farewell.

OPHELIA
O help him you sweet heavens!

HAMLET
If thou dost marry, I'll give thee this plague for thy dowry: be thou as chaste as ice, as pure as snow, thou shalt not escape calumny. Get thee to a nunnery, farewell. Or, if thou wilt needs marry, marry a fool, for wise men know well enough what monsters you make of them. To a nunnery, go, and quickly too. Farewell.

OPHELIA
Heavenly powers restore him!

HAMLET
I have heard of your paintings, too, well enough. God hath given

---

honesty: chastity.
discourse to: familiarity with.
commerce: association, dealings.

sometime: formerly. *paradox:* i.e., a belief not commonly held. *the time:* this present time.

inoculate: improve through the process of grafting or crossbreeding. *relish:* i.e., we will still retain some of our sinful nature.
nunnery: convent/whorehouse. *indifferent:* reasonably.

beck: call, command.

crawling: trapped within our infantile, sinful natures.
arrant: errant, wandering (with a negative connotation).
45

calumny: infamy, malicious accusation. *wilt needs:* must. *monsters:* cuckolds ("monsters" with horns).
50

paintings: cosmetics,

Hamlet points to the woman who was Gertrude in act I.
Hamlet violently pushes Ophelia away from him and exits.

Ophelia, confused and in tears, reaches for the fallen veil, then slumps to the floor and speaks in grief-stricken tones.

The Female Narrator helps Ophelia rise and return to the other women. Furious over Hamlet's self-centered, cruel behavior, the Female Narrator begins to speak. All the men enter, walk to the center of the stage, and watch her silently.
The Female Narrator turns and addresses the women onstage.

Portia steps forward and faces the men. She speaks to Hamlet at first, then to all the others as well.

you one face, and you make yourselves another. You jig, you amble, and you lisp; you nickname God's creatures and make your wantonness your ignorance. Go to, I'll no more on't; it hath made me mad. I say we shall have no more marriage. Those that are married already—all but one—shall live; the rest shall keep as they are. To a nunnery, go.

makeup. You: i.e., You women (in general). *jig:* dance. *amble:* walk suggestively. *you nickname God's creatures:* you behave affectedly. *marriage:* marriages.

OPHELIA
O, what a noble mind is here o'erthrown!
The courtier's, soldier's, scholar's, eye, tongue, sword,
Th' expectancy and rose of the fair state,
The glass of fashion and the mold of form,
Th' observed of all observers—quite, quite down!
And I, of ladies most deject and wretched,
That sucked the honey of his music vows,
Now see that noble and most sovereign reason,
Like sweet bells jangled, out of time and harsh,
That unmatched form and feature of blown youth
Blasted with ecstasy. O, woe is me,
T' have seen what I have seen, see what I see!

Th'expectancy . . . state: The kingdom's greatest and fairest hope. *The glass of fashion:* The mirror of fashion. *the mold of form:* the model for all courtly behavior. *Th'observed of all observers:* The focus of everyone's attention. *deject:* dejected. *blown:* in full bloom. *Blasted with ecstasy:* Withered by madness.

FEMALE NARRATOR
I see a woman may be made a fool,
If she had not a spirit to resist.
Why are our bodies soft and weak and smooth?
Men take women's gifts for impudence.
Speak to him, ladies; see if you can move him.

move: change, convert.

[*The Merchant of Venice,* IV.i]

PORTIA
The quality of mercy is not strained.
It droppeth as the gentle rain from heaven
Upon the place beneath. It is twice blest:
It blesseth him that gives and him that takes.
'Tis mightiest in the mightiest; it becomes
The thronèd monarch better than his crown:
His scepter shows the force of temporal power,
The attribute to awe and majesty,
Wherein doth sit the dread and fear of kings.

strained: constrained, forced.
blest: i.e., it confers a double blessing.
becomes . . . better: is more becoming to

attribute to: outward symbol of.

53–54 *make your wantonness your ignorance:* excuse your indecent behavior by claiming ignorance.

59 *The courtier's . . . sword:* as Ophelia's mind degenerates, so does her syntax. The series would normally read "The courtier's tongue, the soldier's sword, and the scholar's eye."

The Male Narrator is truly impressed by Portia's speech.

As Lady Macbeth gets up and walks toward the group of men, the Male Narrator is affronted by her aggressive behavior.

Lady Macbeth slowly circles the men, looking deeply into each one's face. Finally, she chooses one man and leads him forward. Realizing that he has been chosen, Macbeth speaks to her. The other men retreat to the upstage platforms and sit opposite the women.

But mercy is above this sceptered sway: 10
It is enthroned in the hearts of kings;
It is an attribute to God himself;
And earthly power doth then show likest God's
When mercy seasons justice.   *seasons:* makes more palat-

MALE NARRATOR   able, more mature.
Well said, noble woman. A good lady! We may pick a thousand
salads ere we light on such another herb. What woman is this?
What a sweep of vanity comes this way!

[*Macbeth*, I.vii]

MACBETH
                         How now, what news?

LADY MACBETH
He has almost supped. Why have you left the chamber?   *He:* Duncan, King of Scot-

MACBETH   land. *supped:* finished
Hath he asked for me?   supper.

LADY MACBETH
                  Know you not he has?   *Know you not:* Do you not

MACBETH   know.
We will proceed no further in this business.   5
He hath honored me of late, and I have bought   *bought:* acquired, won.
Golden opinions from all sorts of people,   *sorts:* different kinds.
Which would be worn now in their newest gloss,   *Which:* i.e., his recently
Not cast aside so soon.   gained honor. *would be:*

LADY MACBETH   should be.
                  Was the hope drunk   10
Wherein you dressed yourself? Hath it slept since?
And wakes it now, to look so green and pale   *so green and pale:* so sickly.
At what it did so freely? From this time
Such I account thy love. Art thou afeard
To be the same in thine own act and valor   15
As thou art in desire? Wouldst thou have that
Which thou esteem'st the ornament of life,   *the ornament of life:* i.e.,
And live a coward in thine own esteem,   the crown.
Letting "I dare not" wait upon "I would,"
Like the poor cat i' th'adage?   20

13–14 *From this time . . . love:* If you truly love me, you will show it by killing Duncan.
19–20 *Letting . . . adage:* a popular story in which a cat wished to eat fish, but was reluctant to get her feet wet.

As Lady Macbeth speaks, she slowly begins seducing her husband, kissing and caressing him gently.

They are seated on the floor now, with Macbeth in her arms, his head against her breast.

She leans back into his arms and explains the plan to him.

They kiss passionately.

MACBETH
                    Prithee, peace!
I dare do all that may become a man;
Who dares do more is none.

none: i.e., could not call
himself a "man."

LADY MACBETH
                    What beast was't then
That made you break this enterprise to me?
When you durst do it, then you were a man;
And, to be more than what you were, you would
Be so much more the man. Nor time nor place
Did then adhere, and yet you would make both:
They have made themselves, and that their fitness now
Does unmake you. I have given suck and know
How tender 'tis to love the babe that milks me;
I would, while it was smiling in my face,
Have plucked my nipple from its boneless gums
And dashed the brains out, had I so sworn as you
Have done to this.

break: suggest.
durst: decide to.

Nor . . . nor: Neither . . .
nor. *adhere:* agree, suit our
purpose.
given suck: nursed a child.

the: its.
to this: to do this.

MACBETH
            If we should fail?

LADY MACBETH
                    We fail?
But screw your courage to the sticking place,
And we'll not fail. When Duncan is asleep
(Whereto the rather shall his day's hard journey
Soundly invite him), his two chamberlains
Will I with wine and wassail so convince,
That memory, the warder of the brain,
Shall be a fume, and the receipt of reason
A limbeck only. When in swinish sleep
Their drenched natures lies as in death,
What cannot you and I perform upon
Th'ungarded Duncan? What not put upon
His spongy officers, who shall bear the guilt
Of our great quell?

But: Only (i.e., all you
have to do is).
rather: more readily.
chamberlains: personal
attendants, guards. *wassail:*
drink, celebration. *con-
vince:* overpower. *warder:*
keeper. *receipt of reason:*
the place in which reason
is housed or kept.

spongy: drunken (and
therefore able to have foul

27–28 *And . . . the man:* You will be more than a man (i.e., a king) if you kill Duncan and seize the throne.

29 *yet you would make both:* you were then resolute enough to create your own opportunity (i.e., both the time and the place).

30–31 *They have made themselves . . . you:* The proper conditions have now presented themselves, yet the opportunity to kill Duncan has turned you into a coward.

39 *the sticking place:* a term from archery denoting the notch that held a bowstring taut just prior to shooting.

45 *fume:* strong liquors were thought to cause "fumes" that ascended into the brain, dulling reason and memory.

46 *limbeck:* an "alembic" was a beaker or empty vessel used in alchemical experiments to distill various substances.

As Macbeth and Lady Macbeth are departing, the Male Narrator trails after them and speaks.

While Macbeth and Lady Macbeth recede into the upstage shadows, he returns to the group of men and she to the group of women.

In the background, two women are talking. A flute plays under the women's lines, setting a mood of sadness that reaches one of the men.

The man begins to sing, slowly, wistfully.

MACBETH

             Bring forth men-children only!
For thy undaunted mettle should compose
Nothing but males. Will it not be received,
When we have marked with blood those sleepy two
Of his own chamber, and used their very daggers,
That they have done't?

LADY MACBETH

             Who dares receive it other,
As we shall make our griefs and clamor roar
Upon his death?

MACBETH

             I am settled, and bend up
Each corporal agent to this terrible feat.
Away, and mock the time with fairest show:
False face must hide what the false heart doth know.

MALE NARRATOR

Lady, you are the cruellest she alive. Farewell, fair cruelty. I have
heard her reported to be a woman of an invincible spirit.

FEMALE NARRATOR

And praise we may afford
To any lady that subdues a lord.

QUEEN ELIZABETH

Alas, I am a woman: friendless, hopeless.

QUEEN MARGARET

I am the most unhappy woman living.

deeds pressed upon them).
quell: murder. *undaunted:*
determined, not easily
discouraged. *mettle:*
strength of character. *re-ceived:* accepted as truth.

other: otherwise.

60

bend up: focus, dedicate
(another archery meta-phor). *corporal agent:*
bodily skill. *feat:* deed.
mock the time: deceive the
world. *fairest show:* cheer-ful outward appearance.

70

[*Twelfth Night,* II.iii]

MALE

O mistress mine, where are you roaming?
O stay and hear, your true love's coming,
   That can sing both high and low.
Trip no further, pretty sweeting:
Journeys end in lovers meeting,
   Every wise man's son doth know.

What is love? 'Tis not hereafter;
Present mirth hath present laughter;
   What's to come is still unsure.
In delay there lies no plenty;

sweeting: sweetheart.
in lovers meeting: when
lovers meet.

hereafter: i.e., after we die.

still: always.
plenty: i.e., delay in love

The Narrators sing the last verse with the man. Then all the women join in singing with the two Narrators and the lone male singer.

The Female Narrator speaks to the men and to the audience.

The women's voices attach themselves to the lonely notes of the flute and the Female Narrator's voice. They begin as low keening and open into full-blown mourning. The flute continues playing in the background during this scene. The women stand on the ring of upstage platforms, where they are illuminated by special lights. The rest of the stage is slightly dimmed. These mourning sounds represent the lowest ebb in the evening; each woman is trapped within her sorrow, lamenting her life and her lost loves.

The Duchess sits.

Queen Elizabeth sits.

Then come kiss me, sweet and twenty:
Youth's a stuff will not endure.

BOTH NARRATORS
Youth's a stuff will not endure,
Will not endure, will not endure.

FEMALE NARRATOR
Sorrow concealed, like an oven stopped,
Doth burn the heart to cinders where it is.
Witness the sorrow.

does not bring happiness (*carpe diem* theme). *sweet and twenty:* sweet and twenty times sweeter.

an oven stopped: enclosed (and therefore made hotter).

[*Richard III*, IV.iv]

QUEEN ELIZABETH
Ah, my poor princes! Ah, my tender babes!
My unblown flow'rs, new-appearing sweets!
If yet your gentle souls fly in the air
And be not fixed in doom perpetual,
Hover about me with your airy wings
And hear your mother's lamentation!

unblown: unopened, not yet in bloom. *sweets:* flowers. *doom perpetual:* eternal judgment (in either heaven or hell).

DUCHESS OF YORK
So many miseries have crazed my voice
That my woe-wearied tongue is still and mute.
Edward Plantagenet, why art thou dead?

crazed: tired and cracked through sorrow.
Edward Plantagenet: Edward IV, son to the Duchess of York.

QUEEN ELIZABETH
Wilt thou, O God, fly from such gentle lambs
And throw them in the entrails of the wolf?
When didst thou sleep when such a deed was done?

QUEEN MARGARET
When holy Harry died, and my sweet son.

When didst: Whenever in the past did.
holy Harry: Henry VI, husband to Margaret. *my sweet son:* Edward, Prince of Wales, husband to Lady Anne. *mortal living ghost:* a ghost doomed to live forever. *grave's due by life usurped:* i.e., one who had lived too long. *abstract:* general example or epitome. *thou:* the earth. *afford:* provide.

DUCHESS OF YORK
Dead life, blind sight, poor mortal living ghost;
Woe's scene, world's shame, grave's due by life usurped;
Brief abstract and record of tedious days:
Rest thy unrest on England's lawful earth,
Unlawfully made drunk with innocent blood!

QUEEN ELIZABETH
Ah, that thou wouldst as soon afford a grave
As thou canst yield a melancholy seat!
Then would I hide my bones, not rest them here.
Ah, who hath any cause to mourn but we?

1 *my poor princes:* Edward, Prince of Wales (later King Edward V), and Richard, Duke of York, both murdered in the Tower of London by order of Richard III.

In her sorrow, Queen Margaret turns angrily on the other women.

The three women continue their keening in lower tones, all three simultaneously repeating their litany of losses. The notes of the flute accompany them as the lights fade down and then fade up on two approaching women: the Queen and her Lady-in-waiting. The flute continues with a melancholy tune, as do the low sounds of the three mourning women.

The Queen and her Lady try to find a way to overcome their own sadness and the sounds of mourning that surround them.

QUEEN MARGARET
If ancient sorrow be most reverend,
Give mine the benefit of seniory,
And let my griefs frown on the upper hand.
If sorrow can admit society,
Tell o'er your woes again by viewing mine:
I had an Edward, till a Richard killed him;
I had a husband, till a Richard killed him.
Thou hadst an Edward, till a Richard killed him;
Thou hadst a Richard, till a Richard killed him.
DUCHESS OF YORK
I had a Richard too, and thou didst kill him;
I had a Rutland too; thou holp'st to kill him.
QUEEN MARGARET
Thou hadst a Clarence too, and Richard killed him.
From forth the kennel of thy womb hath crept
A hell-hound that doth hunt us all to death.
That dog, that had his teeth before his eyes
To worry lambs and lap their gentle blood,
That foul defacer of God's handiwork,
That excellent grand tyrant of the earth
That reigns in galled eyes of weeping souls,
Thy womb let loose to chase us to our graves.
O upright, just, and true-disposing God,
How do I thank thee, that this carnal cur
Preys on the issue of his mother's body,
And makes her pew-fellow with others' moan!
DUCHESS OF YORK
O Harry's wife, triumph not in my woes!
God witness with me, I have wept for thine.

ancient: of longest duration. *seniory:* seniority. *frown . . . hand:* i.e., in the position of most nobility. *admit:* permit. *Tell o'er:* Remember (by listening to my story). *Edward:* her son, the Prince of Wales. *Richard:* Richard III. *husband:* King Henry VI. *Thou/Thou:* Queen Elizabeth. *Edward:* Edward V. *Richard:* the young Duke of York. *Richard:* Duke of York, husband to the Duchess. *Rutland:* Edmund, son of the Duke of York. *holp'st:* helped. *Clarence:* George, Duke of Clarence, brother to Richard III. *teeth:* according to popular folklore, Richard had been born with teeth. *worry:* rip to pieces/ frighten. *excellent:* without peer (ironic). *galled:* red and swollen from crying. *carnal cur:* deadly dog. *pew-fellow:* companion.

[*Richard II*, III.iv]

QUEEN
What sport shall we devise here in this garden
To drive away the heavy thought of care?
LADY
Madam, we'll play at bowls.
QUEEN
'Twill make me think the world is full of rubs,
And that my fortune runs against the bias.

bowls: lawn bowling.

rubs: obstacles in lawn bowling. *bias:* grain (either

45 *Preys on the issue of his mother's body:* i.e., Kills his own mother's children.

The Lady begins to sing the "Willow" song (she will become Desdemona in the next scene).

The three mourning women end their keening.

The music from the flute fades out. The women cross upstage together, all holding hands to help endure their sorrow. During their cross, Desdemona runs to Iago and pulls him forward.

LADY
Madam, we'll dance.

QUEEN
My legs can keep no measure in delight,
When my poor heart no measure keeps in grief.
Therefore, no dancing, girl. Some other sport.

LADY
Madam, we'll tell tales.

QUEEN
Of sorrow or of joy?

LADY
              Of either, madam.

QUEEN
Of neither, girl.
For if of joy, being altogether wanting,
It doth remember me the more of sorrow;
Or if of grief, being altogether had,
It adds more sorrow to my want of joy:
For what I have, I need not to repeat;
And what I want, it boots not to complain.

LADY
Madam, I'll sing.

QUEEN
        'Tis well that thou hast cause;
But thou shouldst please me better, wouldst thou weep.

LADY
I could weep, madam, would it do you good.

QUEEN
And I could sing, would weeping do me good,
And never borrow any tear of thee.

DUCHESS OF YORK
Is not my sorrow deep, having no bottom?
Then be my passion bottomless.

contrary to the natural slope of the earth" or *"against the weighted side of the ball").* measure: rhythm (a "measure" was a slow, formal dance). *measure:* moderation. 10

wanting: lacking. *remember:* remind.

want: lack.

boots not: is useless.

20

sing: i.e., for joy. *would weeping:* if weeping would. *And never borrow any tear of thee:* And never ask you to cry for me (cf. line 23).

[*Othello*, IV.ii]

DESDEMONA
            Alas, Iago,
What shall I do to win my lord again?
Good friend, go to him; for by this light of heaven,
I know not how I lost him. Here I kneel:

Iago backs away from Desdemona,and Emilia escorts her forward.

Emilia sets up two chairs for herself and Desdemona. The two women seem to find comfort talking with each other.

Desdemona begins to loosen a sash that is tied tightly around her waist.

Desdemona asks Emilia to unclasp her necklace.

If e'er my will did trespass 'gainst his love—
Either in discourse of thought or actual deed,
Or that mine eyes, mine ears, or any sense
Delighted them in any other form,
Or that I do not yet, and ever did,
And ever will (though he do shake me off
To beggarly divorcement) love him dearly—
Comfort forswear me! Unkindness may do much,
And his unkindness may defeat my life,
But never taint my love. I cannot say "whore":
It does abhor me now I speak the word;
To do the act that might the addition earn,
Not the world's mass of vanity could make me.

will: passion, sexual appetite. *discourse of thought:*
the process of thinking.
them: i.e., delighted themselves (by being infatuated
with). *any other form:*
another man.

defeat: destroy.
taint: diminish, sully.
now: now that.
addition: title.
the world's mass of vanity:
all the valuable objects in
this world that reflect
pride.

[*Othello*, IV.iii]

EMILIA
How goes it now? He looks gentler than he did.

DESDEMONA
He says he will return incontinent,
And hath commanded me to go to bed,
And bade me to dismiss you.

incontinent: immediately.

EMILIA
                          Dismiss me?

5

DESDEMONA
It was his bidding. Therefore, good Emilia,
Give me my nightly wearing, and adieu.
We must not now displease him.

nightly wearing: night-
gown.

EMILIA
I would you had never seen him!

DESDEMONA
So would not I. My love doth so approve him,
That even his stubbornness, his checks, his frowns—
Prithee unpin me—have grace and favor in them.

approve: i.e., I love even
his faults. *checks:* criti-
cisms. *favor:* attractiveness.

EMILIA
I have laid those sheets you bade me on the bed.

bade: asked.

5–12 *If e'er . . . me:* this complex parenthetical construction serves to qualify and expand upon a single enveloping thought—"If e'er my will did trespass 'gainst his love . . . [then] Comfort forswear me!" The internal rationale seems divided into three either/or clauses: If I ever trespassed, 1) either in thought or deed, or 2) by being interested in another man, or 3) because I do not, did not, nor will not continue to love Othello dearly, then comfort forswear me.

Emilia brushes Desdemona's long hair. Faint music from the flute can be heard offstage.

Emilia helps Desdemona remove her earrings and bracelet.
Desdemona deliberately changes the subject to lighten the mood. Emilia immediately joins in the attempt to cheer up her mistress.

Desdemona begins singing the tune that has been in her head all evening. The flute accompanies her.

DESDEMONA
All's one. Good faith, how foolish are our minds.
If I do die before thee, prithee shroud me
In one of those same sheets.

EMILIA
                              Come, come, you talk.

DESDEMONA
My mother had a maid called Barbary;
She was in love, and he she loved proved mad
And did forsake her. She had a song of "Willow."
An old thing 'twas, but it expressed her fortune,
And she died singing it. That song tonight
Will not go from my mind; I have much to do
But to go hang my head all at one side
And sing it like poor Barbary. Prithee, dispatch.

EMILIA
Shall I go fetch your nightgown?

DESDEMONA
                              No, unpin me here.
This Lodovico is a proper man.

EMILIA
                              A very handsome man.

DESDEMONA
He speaks well.

EMILIA
I know a lady in Venice would have walked barefoot to Palestine for a touch of his nether lip.

DESDEMONA

  "The poor soul sat sighing by a sycamore tree,
    Sing all a Green willow;
  Her hand on her bosom, her head on her knee,
    Sing willow, willow, willow.
  The fresh streams ran by her and murmured her moans,
    Sing willow, willow, willow;
  Her salt tears fell from her and softened the stones,
    Sing willow, willow, willow—"
Prithee, hie thee; he'll come anon.
  "Sing all a green willow must be my garland.

All's one: It doesn't make any difference. *shroud:* the winding sheet with which corpses were wrapped prior to burial. *you talk:* i.e., how foolishly you talk!

mad: unfaithful/insane (?). *Willow:* symbol of lost love.

dispatch: hurry and finish.

Lodovico: a handsome, noble Venetian recently arrived in Venice.

30

nether: lower.

35

murmured: echoed.

40
hie thee: hurry.

23–25 *I have . . . Barbary:* It's all I can do to keep from hanging my head to one side and singing this song as Barbary did.

Emilia joins Desdemona in singing the last verse.

The two women cuddle up with one another for comfort and support.

Let nobody blame him; his scorn I approve—"
Nay, that's not next. Hark! Who is't that knocks?

EMILIA
It's the wind.   45

DESDEMONA
"I called my love 'false love'; but what said he then?
     Sing willow, willow, willow;
   If I court moe women, you'll couch with moe men—"   *moe:* more.
So, get thee gone. Good night. Mine eyes do itch;
Doth that bode weeping?   50

EMILIA
                   'Tis neither here nor there.   *'Tis neither here nor there:*
                                                           It doesn't mean anything.

DESDEMONA
I have heard it said so. O, these men, these men!
Dost thou in conscience think—tell me, Emilia—   *in conscience:* honestly.
That there be women do abuse their husbands
In such gross kind?   *In such gross kind:* i.e., By
                                                          being unfaithful.

EMILIA
There be some such; no question.

DESDEMONA
Wouldst thou do such a deed for all the world?

EMILIA
Why? Would not you?

DESDEMONA
                   No, by this heavenly light.

EMILIA
Nor I neither by this heavenly light;   60
I might do't as well i' th' dark.

DESDEMONA
Wouldst thou do such a deed for all the world?

EMILIA
The world's a huge thing. It is a great price   *price:* prize, payment.
For a small vice.

DESDEMONA
Good troth, I think thou wouldst not.   *Good troth:* In good truth.

EMILIA
By my troth, I think I should, and undo it when I had done.
Marry, I would not do such a thing for a joint-ring, nor for mea-   *joint-ring:* an inexpensive
sures of lawn, nor for gowns, petticoats, nor caps, nor any petty   ring made in two halves,
exhibition. But for all the world! God's pity, who would not   which were then joined
make her husband a cuckold to make him a monarch? I should   together. *measures of lawn:*
venture purgatory for it.   bolts of fine linen. *petty*

Emilia warms to her theme and lets out her own feelings about being victimized by men.

Desdemona and Emilia begin to exit.

The Female Narrator helps them offstage. Turning, she speaks to the Male Narrator.

The Male Narrator is moved by these scenes of sorrow to admire the strength in women.

The Female Narrator changes to a teasing mood.

DESDEMONA

I do not think there is any such woman.

EMILIA

Yes, a dozen, and as many to th'vantage as would store the
world they played for.
But I do think it is their husbands' faults
If wives do fall. Say that they slack their duties
And pour our treasures into foreign laps,
Or else break out in peevish jealousies,
Throwing restraint upon us. Or say they strike us,
Or scant our former having in despite.
Why, we have galls, and though we have some grace,
Yet have we some revenge. Let husbands know
Their wives have sense like them: they see and smell
And have their palates for both sweet and sour,
As husbands have. What is it that they do
When they change us for others? Is it sport?
I think it is. And doth affection breed it?
I think it doth. Is't frailty that thus errs?
It is so too. And have not we affections?
Desires for sport? and frailty, as men have?
Then let them use us well; else let them know,
The ills we do, their ills instruct us so.

DESDEMONA

Good night, good night. God me such uses send,
Not to pick bad from bad, but by bad mend!

FEMALE NARRATOR

Thy heart is big; get thee apart and weep.
Why stand we like soft-hearted women here, wailing our
losses?

MALE NARRATOR

Sorrow that is couched in seeming gladness
Is like that mirth fate turns to sudden sadness.

FEMALE NARRATOR

You know I am a woman, lacking wit
To make a seemly answer.

exhibition: insignificant
fact. *venture:* risk going to.

to th'vantage: in addition.
store: populate with children.
slack: do not perform
properly (with a sexual
pun). *duties:* marriage
vows and responsibilities.
pour . . . laps: make love
to other women. *throwing
restraint upon us:* watching
us too closely. *galls:* the
capacity to feel insults and
injuries. *sense:* sensual
feelings. *palates:* appetites.
others: other women.
errs: commits an error.

90
use: treat.

uses: practices, habits.

95

couched: hidden, con-
cealed. *that mirth:* that
mirth which.
100
seemly: proper.

---

80 *scant our former having in despite:* reduce our household allowance (or make love with us less frequently) in
order to spite us.

92 *The ills we do, their ills instruct us so:* We learn our bad behavior by observing theirs.

93 *God me such uses send:* May God make it my custom.

94 *Not to pick . . . mend:* Not to mimic men's bad conduct, but to shun evil and strive for its spiritual opposite.

He answers jovially.

The Female Narrator crosses upstage, throws off her shoes, and lets down her hair. Having waited all evening to show her truly passionate spirit, she now becomes Cleopatra.

Charmian advances to the Male Narrator and the other men, then she sets up two chairs for Cleopatra's "throne." The Male Narrator selects one man from the group and pushes him into center stage where he becomes the Messenger. Everyone on stage moves back a little to leave room for Cleopatra and the poor Messenger, who has now been abandoned by the other men. Charmian stands apart from the action with the Male Narrator.

Cleopatra attempts to hold back her fury, but she can not resist turning on the Messenger again before he has a chance to speak.

MALE NARRATOR
Peace, foolish woman.
FEMALE NARRATOR
I will not peace.
MALE NARRATOR
Come, give us a taste of your quality; come, a passionate speech.
FEMALE NARRATOR
Sweet partner, I must not yet forsake you.   105
CHARMIAN
Here comes the lady, in the very torrent, tempest, and, as I may
say, the whirlwind of passion.

[*Antony and Cleopatra,* II.v]

CLEOPATRA
                                O, from Italy!
Ram thou thy fruitful tidings in mine ears,
That long time have been barren.
MESSENGER
                        Madam, madam—
CLEOPATRA
Antonio's dead! If thou say so, villain,   5   *but:* but if he is.
Thou killest thy mistress; but well and free,   *yield:* describe.
If thou so yield him, there is gold, and here,
My bluest veins to kiss: a hand that kings
Have lipped, and trembled kissing.   *lipped:* kissed.
MESSENGER
First, madam, he is well.   10
CLEOPATRA
Why, there's more gold. But, sirrah, mark: we use   *mark:* listen, pay attention.
To say the dead are well. Bring it to that,   *well:* well off (being dead).
The gold I give thee will I melt and pour   *Bring it to that:* i.e., If
Down thy ill-uttering throat.   you tell me Antony is dead.
MESSENGER
Good madam, hear me.   15
CLEOPATRA
                        Well, go to; I will.
I have a mind to strike thee ere thou speak'st.   *ere:* before.
Yet, if thou say Antony lives, is well,

2–3 *Ram . . . barren:* Quickly tell your good news to my ears, which have been without knowledge of Antony for a
long time (note the abundant sexual imagery in "Ram," "fruitful," and "barren").

The Messenger attempts a weak joke. He is terrified.

Cleopatra strikes the Messenger.

She pushes him to the ground by pulling on his hair.

I'll set thee in a shower of gold, and hail
Rich pearls upon thee.

MESSENGER

            Madam, he's well.

CLEOPATRA

Make thee a fortune from me.

MESSENGER

             But yet, madam—

CLEOPATRA

I do not like "but yet": it does allay
The good precedence. Fie upon "but yet!"
"But yet" is as a jailer to bring forth
Some monstrous malefactor. Prithee, friend,
Pour out the pack of matter to mine ear—
The good and bad together. Antony's
In state of health, thou say'st, and thou say'st free.

MESSENGER

Free, madam? No. I made no such report.
He's bound unto Octavia.

CLEOPATRA

           For what good turn?

MESSENGER

For the best turn i'th'bed.

CLEOPATRA

           I am pale, Charmian.

MESSENGER

Madam, he's married to Octavia.

CLEOPATRA

The most infectious pestilence upon thee!

MESSENGER

Good madam, patience.

CLEOPATRA

          What say you? Hence,
Horrible villain, or I'll spurn thine eyes
Like balls before me! I'll unhair thy head!
Thou shalt be whipped with wire and stewed in brine,
Smarting in ling'ring pickle!

MESSENGER

           Gracious madam,
I that do bring the news made not the match.

CLEOPATRA

Say 'tis not so, a province I will give thee,

---

hail: shower.
20

Make thee: O, you will make.

allay / The good precedence: discredit the good news which came before.
malefactor: evildoer.
Pour . . . ear: Tell me all your news at once.
30

Octavia: Caesar's sister.

35

spurn: kick.

pickle: pickling solution.

match: i.e., the marriage between Antony and Octavia.

Cleopatra, now absolutely furious, advances on the Messenger.

The Messenger retreats to the group of men.

Charmian steps forward and tries to reason with Cleopatra.

Charmian goes to the men, seizes the reluctant Messenger by the arm, and brings him back to Cleopatra.

Cleopatra tries to relax by stretching out her legs on both chairs as she sits on her throne.

And make thy fortunes proud; the blow thou hadst
Shall make thy peace for moving me to rage,
And I will boot thee with what gift beside
Thy modesty can beg.

boot thee: present you.
what: whatever. *beside:* in
addition. *modesty:* moderate appetite for riches.

MESSENGER

            He's married, madam.

CLEOPATRA

Rogue, thou hast lived too long!

MESSENGER

                    Nay, then I'll run.

What mean you, madam? I have made no fault.

CHARMIAN

Good madam, keep yourself within yourself;
The man is innocent.

keep yourself within yourself: calm down (remember
your high rank).

CLEOPATRA

Some innocents scape not the thunderbolt.
Melt Egypt into Nile! And kindly creatures
Turn all to serpents! Call the slave again:
Though I am mad, I will not bite him. Call!

thunderbolt: punishment
of the gods.

60

CHARMIAN

He is afeard to come.

afeard: afraid.

CLEOPATRA

            I will not hurt him.

These hands do lack nobility, that they strike
A meaner than myself, since I myself
Have given myself the cause. Come hither, sir.
Though it be honest, it is never good
To bring bad news.

that: if.

A meaner: someone of
lower rank
the cause: i.e., her love for
Antony.

MESSENGER

         I have done my duty.

CLEOPATRA

Is he married?
I cannot hate thee worser than I do
If thou again say "yes."

70

MESSENGER

          He's married, madam.

CLEOPATRA

The gods confound thee! Dost thou hold there still?

confound: destroy. *hold*

47–48 *the blow . . . rage:* i.e., I've already punished you for angering me; I won't strike you again.

58–59 *Melt Egypt . . . serpents:* Cleopatra's epic curse implies that the world has turned upside down: even the
messenger, who should be a "kindly creature," has changed into a "serpent."

Cleopatra pulls his face very close to hers.

The Messenger, with no gold for his trouble, hurries back to the group of men. He is happy to be free of Cleopatra's wrath.

The Male Narrator, who is visibly shaken after viewing the last scene, describes Cleopatra to the other men.

Cleopatra walks upstage and stands on the upper platforms, center, illuminated by a dim spotlight.

The Male Narrator turns to the other men.

Enobarbus, Maecenas, and Agrippa have been watching Cleopatra in awe (and a bit of terror). Viewing her passion and energy has helped revive them from their weakened, hung-over condition.

MESSENGER
Should I lie, madam?
CLEOPATRA
              O, I would thou didst,
So half my Egypt were submerged and made
A cistern for scaled snakes! Go, get thee hence!
Hadst thou Narcissus in thy face, to me
Thou wouldst appear most ugly. He is married?
MESSENGER
I crave your Highness' pardon.
CLEOPATRA
              He is married?
MESSENGER
Take no offense that I would not offend you;
To punish me for what you make me do
Seems much unequal. He's married to Octavia.
CLEOPATRA
O, that his fault should make a knave of thee,
That art not what th'art sure of! Get thee hence.
The merchandise which thou hast brought from Rome
Are all too dear for me. Lie they upon thy hand,
And be undone by 'em!
MALE NARRATOR
             Affliction, passion, hell itself,
She turns to favor and prettiness.
CLEOPATRA
Sigh no more, ladies, sigh no more;
Men were deceivers ever.
MALE NARRATOR
Kindness in women, not their beauteous looks,
Shall win my love.

there still: persist with the same bad news.

75
So: Even though.
cistern: a large reservoir of water.

80

much unequal: quite unjust.
85

merchandise: news.
dear: expensive, costly.

90

95

[*Antony and Cleopatra*, II.ii]

MAECENAS
She's a most triumphant lady, if report be square to her.

square to: accurate con-

---

78 *Narcissus:* a beautiful Greek youth who fell in love with his own reflection in a pool of water.

82 *Take no offense . . . you:* Do not be offended by my hesitancy in answering you.

85–86 *O, that his fault . . . sure of:* How ironic that Antony's marriage (his "fault") should make you a knave, you who aren't guilty of the sin you report.

88–89 *Lie they . . . undone by 'em:* i.e., May you never profit from having brought such bad news.

Agrippa and Maecenas gaze upstage at Cleopatra. Enobarbus does not look at her. He faces them as he tells his story. The atmosphere is very still and quiet, as if they were onstage alone. The Male Narrator and the Fifth Male join the three on stage. All of them are enthralled by Enobarbus' description of this extraordinary woman.

ENOBARBUS
When she first met Mark Antony, she pursed up his heart, upon
the river of Cydnus.

AGRIPPA
There she appeared indeed, or my reporter devised well for her.

ENOBARBUS
I will tell you.
The barge she sat in, like a burnished throne,
Burnt on the water; the poop was beaten gold;
Purple the sails, and so perfumed that
The winds were love-sick with them; the oars were silver,
Which to the tune of flutes kept stroke, and made
The water which they beat to follow faster,
As amorous of their strokes. For her own person,
It beggared all description: she did lie
In her pavilion, cloth-of-gold of tissue
O'erpicturing that Venus where we see
The fancy outwork nature. On each side her
Stood pretty dimpled boys, like smiling Cupids,
With divers-colored fans, whose wind did seem
To glow the delicate cheeks which they did cool,
And what they undid did.

AGRIPPA
                    O, rare for Antony!

ENOBARBUS
Her gentlewomen, like the Nereides,
So many mermaids, tended her i' th'eyes
And made their bends adornings. At the helm,
A seeming mermaid steers. The silken tackle
Swell with the touches of those flower-soft hands
That yarely frame the office. From the barge,
A strange invisible perfume hits the sense
Of the adjacent wharfs. The city cast
Her people out upon her; and Antony,

cerning.
pursed up: pocketed.

devised well: fabricated
nicely.
        5

poop: the highest deck of
her ship, probably at the
stern.
10

As: As if they were. *For:*
As for.

15
her: of her.

divers: various.
glow: cause to glow.
20

Nereides: nymphs of the
sea.
*made their bends adorn-
ings:* bowed adoringly.
tackle: ship's rigging and
sails. *yarely frame the
office:* skillfully perform
the job (of tending the
sails). *hits the sense:* is

3 *the river of Cydnus:* a river in the ancient region of Cilicia, which now comprises part of southern Turkey. The area was ruled for a while by the Ptolemaic kings of Egypt, then later became part of the Roman Empire.

14 *cloth-of-gold of tissue:* cloth composed of gold and silken threads woven together.

15–16 *O'erpicturing that Venus . . . nature:* Outdoing the famous picture of Venus (by Apelles) in which the painter's art was said to be more beautiful than nature.

23 *tended her i' th' eyes:* this obscure phrase may mean that Cleopatra's women waited on her openly, in full view of everyone, or that the women responded quickly, even to her most subtle glances.

29–30 *The city . . . her:* i.e., Everyone in the city rushed to the wharf to see Cleopatra's barge.

Agrippa shares this bit of gossip with the other men.

All of the men feel refreshed by these stories about Cleopatra. They each continue to talk about their loved ones.

One man, proud of his lover in spite of the fact that she is no Cleopatra, shows the other men her picture.

Enthroned in the market place, did sit alone,
Whistling to th'air, which, but for vacancy,
Had gone to gaze on Cleopatra too,
And made a gap in nature.

AGRIPPA
　　　　　　　　　　　　Rare Egyptian! 　　　　　35
She made great Caesar lay his sword to bed;
he ploughed her, and she cropped.

ENOBARBUS
　　　　　　　　　　　　I saw her once
Hop forty paces through the public street;
And having lost her breath, she spoke, and panted, 　40
That she did make defect perfection
And, breathless, power breathe forth.

MAECENAS
Now Antony must leave her utterly.

ENOBARBUS
Never. He will not.
Age cannot wither her, nor custom stale
Her infinite variety. Other women cloy
The appetites they feed, but she makes hungry
Where most she satisfies; for vilest things
Become themselves in her, that the holy priests
Bless her when she is riggish.

MALE NARRATOR
Her passions are made of nothing but the finest part of true love.

AGRIPPA
Age cannot wither her, nor custom stale
Her infinite variety.

MAECENAS
Thou, Julia, thou hast metamorphised me.

<h2 style="text-align:center">[Sonnet 130]</h2>

SECOND MALE
My mistress' eyes are nothing like the sun;
Coral is far more red than her lips' red;
If snow be white, why then her breasts are dun;

---

perceptible. Of: On.

ploughed: made love with.
cropped: bore fruit (gave birth to a son).
Hop: Run.

utterly: completely, totally.

stale: make stale.
cloy: nauseate through excess.

Become themselves: Are attractive, becoming. *riggish:* lustful.

metamorphised me: changed me completely.

nothing: not at all.

dun: brown.

---

32 *but for vacancy:* except that it would have created a vacuum (cf. "gap in nature," line 34).
36 *Caesar:* Julius Caesar, with whom Cleopatra had a son (Caesarion).
41 *That . . . perfection:* i.e., She made even being out of breath look perfectly beautiful.

The men retire to the platforms to dream of their loves, while Romeo stays behind and looks longingly at Juliet (who has just been revealed at center on the platforms). Romeo is below her, at stage level.
The Male Narrator looks up at Juliet and describes her.

Thinking she is alone, Juliet speaks out about the man she loves.
Hearing his name, Romeo hides close to the audience (behind one of the chairs).

Romeo turns to the other men and asks this question in a whisper. They hush him.

Romeo stands up abruptly and shouts to Juliet.

Juliet rushes for cover behind the women.

If hairs be wires, black wires grow on her head.
I have seen roses damasked, red and white,
But no such roses see I in her cheeks;
And in some perfumes is there more delight
Than in the breath that from my mistress reeks.
I love to hear her speak, yet well I know
That music hath a far more pleasing sound;
I grant I never saw a goddess go:
My mistress, when she walks, treads on the ground.
      And yet, by heaven, I think my love as rare
      As any she belied with false compare.
MALE NARRATOR
Vouchsafe, divine perfection of a woman.

damasked: mixed red and white.

reeks: breathes (without our twentieth-century negative connotation). *go:* walk.

rare: extraordinary. *any she:* any other woman. *belied:* lied about or misrepresented (with overblown praise). *compare:* comparison. *Vouchsafe:* Permit, allow me.

[*Romeo and Juliet*, II.ii]

JULIET
O Romeo, Romeo! Wherefore art thou Romeo?
Deny thy father and refuse thy name;
Or, if thou wilt not, be but sworn my love,
And I'll no longer be a Capulet.
ROMEO
Shall I hear more, or shall I speak at this?   5
JULIET
'Tis but thy name that is my enemy;
Thou art thyself, though not a Montague.
What's Montague? It is nor hand nor foot,
Nor arm, nor face, nor any other part
Belonging to a man. O, be some other name!
What's in a name? That which we call a rose
By any other word would smell as sweet:
So Romeo would, were he not Romeo called,
Retain that dear perfection which he owes
Without that title. Romeo, doff thy name;
And for thy name, which is no part of thee,
Take all myself.
ROMEO
            I take thee at thy word!
Call me but "love," and I'll be new baptized;
Henceforth I never will be Romeo.   20
JULIET
What man art thou that thus bescreened in night
So stumblest on my counsel?

Wherefore art thou Romeo: Why are you [named] Romeo?

though not a Montague: even if you take some family name other than "Montague." *nor . . . nor:* neither . . . nor.

owes: owns. *doff:* take off (like a cap).

bescreened in: hidden or obscured by. *counsel:* secret

Romeo tries to entice Juliet back again.

Juliet peeks out from behind the women, then slowly returns to center.

Romeo, now full of courage, draws her shyness out of her.

Juliet comes as close to him as she dares, using the edge of darkness as her protection.

ROMEO
               By a name
I know not how to tell thee who I am.
My name, dear saint, is hateful to myself
Because it is an enemy to thee;
Had I it written, I would tear the word.

JULIET
My ears have not yet drunk a hundred words
Of thy tongue's uttering, yet I know the sound:
Art thou not Romeo and a Montague?

ROMEO
Neither, fair maid, if either thee dislike.

JULIET
How camest thou hither, tell me, and wherefore?
The orchard walls are high and hard to climb,
And the place death, considering who thou art,
If any of my kinsmen find thee here.

ROMEO
With love's light wings did I o'erperch these walls;
For stony limits cannot hold love out,
And what love can do, that dares love attempt:
Therefore thy kinsmen are no stop to me.

JULIET
If they do see thee, they will murder thee.

ROMEO
Alack, there lies more peril in thine eye
Than twenty of their swords! Look thou but sweet,
And I am proof against their enmity.

JULIET
By whose direction found'st thou out this place?

ROMEO
By love, that first did prompt me to inquire;
He lent me counsel, and I lent him eyes.

JULIET
Thou knowest the mask of night is on my face,
Else would a maiden blush bepaint my cheek
For that which thou hast heard me speak tonight.
Fain would I dwell on form—fain, fain deny

thoughts.

25

if either thee dislike: if you
dislike either of these
names. *wherefore:* why.

And the place death: i.e.,
You will be killed.

o'erperch: fly over.

And . . . attempt: Whatever
love is able to do, love will
attempt. *stop:* hindrance.

40

sweet: sweetly.
proof: protected. *enmity:*
hatred.

45

Fain: Gladly. *compliment:*

---

25 *dear saint:* a reference to the "pilgrim" sonnet (*Romeo and Juliet,* I.v. 94–107), in which Romeo describes his love for Juliet in terms of the adoration of saints. Since the earlier conversation took place at a masked ball, this present scene is the first opportunity Juliet has had to see Romeo's face.

What I have spoke. But farewell compliment!
Dost thou love me? I know thou wilt say "ay,"
And I will take thy word. Yet, if thou swear'st,
Thou mayst prove false. At lovers' perjuries,
They say Jove laughs. O gentle Romeo,
If thou dost love, pronounce it faithfully;
Of, if thou thinkest I am too quickly won,
I'll frown and be perverse and say thee "nay,"
So thou wilt woo, but else not for the world.
In truth, fair Montague, I am too fond,
And therefore thou mayst think my 'havior light;
But trust me, gentleman: I'll prove more true
Than those that have more cunning to be strange.
I should have been more strange, I must confess,
But that thou overheard'st, ere I was ware,
My true-love passion. Therefore, pardon me,
And not impute this yielding to light love,
Which the dark night hath so discovered.

ROMEO
Lady, by yonder blessed moon I vow,
That tips with silver all these fruit-tree tops—

JULIET
O, swear not by the moon, th'inconstant moon,
That monthly changes in her circled orb,
Lest that thy love prove likewise variable.

ROMEO
What shall I swear by?

JULIET
              Do not swear at all.
Or, if thou wilt, swear by thy gracious self,
Which is the god of my idolatry,
And I'll believe thee.

ROMEO
           If my heart's dear love—

JULIET
Well, do not swear. Although I joy in thee,
I have no joy of this contract tonight:
It is too rash, too unadvised, too sudden;
Too like the lightning, which doth cease to be
Ere one can say "It lightens." Sweet, good night!

coyness and proper manners.

perjuries: lies (especially under oath, as Romeo is about to swear).

fond: foolish.
'havior: behavior.
light: frivolous, lacking in modesty.

ere: before. *ware:* aware (of your presence).
this yielding: my sudden declaration of love. *light:* of little value. *discovered:* revealed.
70

her circled orb: the orbit of her sphere. *variable:* changeable.

75
if thou wilt: i.e., if you must swear. *god of my idolatry:* god that I worship.

80
of: in. *contract:* exchange of lovers' vows.

---

59 *but else not for the world:* i.e., the only reason I would be coy is if you feel I'm being won too easily; otherwise, I would not do so for the whole world.

Juliet begins to leave.

Romeo cries out to her.

She admonishes him.

He pulls her back and makes a formal request.

The Nurse (Female Narrator) calls "Madam" from the side of the stage.
The Nurse calls again. Juliet snaps at the Nurse, then exits toward the group of women.

Thinking Juliet has left for the night, Romeo returns to the other men.

Juliet runs back up center, looking for Romeo.

At first, she whispers his name. Then she shouts.

Romeo rushes back to center stage.

They stand silently for a moment, looking at each other. The lights come up slowly as dawn is breaking.

This bud of love, by summer's ripening breath,   85
May prove a beauteous flow'r when next we meet.
Good night, good night! As sweet repose and rest
Come to thy heart as that within my breast.   *that:* i.e., the contentment.

ROMEO
O, wilt thou leave me so unsatisfied?

JULIET
What satisfaction canst thou have tonight?   90

ROMEO
Th'exchange of thy love's faithful vow for mine.

JULIET
I gave thee mine before thou didst request it;
And yet I would it were to give again.   *it were:* it were mine.

ROMEO
Wouldst thou withdraw it? For what purpose, love?

JULIET
But to be frank and give it thee again.   *frank:* generous/candid,
And yet I wish but for the thing I have.   honest.
My bounty is as boundless as the sea,   *bounty:* generosity.
My love as deep; the more I give to thee,
The more I have, for both are infinite.   100
I hear some noise within. Dear love, adieu!
Anon, good nurse!—Sweet Montague, be true.   *Anon:* Right away.

ROMEO
O blessed, blessed night! I am afeard,   *afeard:* afraid.
Being in night, all this is but a dream,   *Being in:* Since this is.
Too flattering-sweet to be substantial.   105

JULIET
Hist! Romeo, hist! O, for a falc'ner's voice   *A falc'ner's voice:* the
To lure this tassel-gentle back again.   strong voice of a man who
Romeo!   keeps and calls falcons.
                                                              tassel-gentle: a male pere-
ROMEO   grine falcon, used princi-
        My sweet?   pally by nobles.

JULIET   110
I have forgot why I did call thee back.

ROMEO
Let me stand here till thou remember it.

JULIET
I shall forget, to have thee still stand there,
Remem'bring how I love thy company.

ROMEO
And I'll still stay, to have thee still forget,
Forgetting any other home but this.   115

Juliet slowly returns to the group of women.

The Male Narrator speaks as Romeo walks back to the group of men.

Cordelia comes toward the men, searching for her father. The two men look directly at Cordelia as they describe her.

Lear has fallen asleep after the long evening's party. Cordelia sits with him and cradles him in her arms.

JULIET
'Tis almost morning. I would have thee gone,
And yet no farther than a wanton's bird,
That lets it hop a little from his hand,
Like a poor prisoner in his twisted gyves,
And with a silken thread plucks it back again,
So loving-jealous of his liberty.

ROMEO
I would I were thy bird.

JULIET
                              Sweet, so would I;
Yet I would kill thee with much cherishing.
Good night, good night! Parting is such sweet sorrow,
That I shall say "good night" till it be morrow.

ROMEO
Sleep dwell upon thine eyes, peace in thy breast;
Would I were sleep and peace, so sweet to rest.

MALE NARRATOR
Having such a blessing in his lady,
He finds the joys of heaven here on earth.

SECOND MALE
She's a most exquisite lady!

KENT
                              Her voice was ever soft,
Gentle, and low: an excellent thing in woman.

wanton's: a spoiled child's (with, perhaps, a secondary reference to Cupid). *gyves:* chains.
his: its.

125

Would: I wish. *so sweet to rest:* to have such a sweet place in which to rest.
130

[*King Lear,* IV.vii]

CORDELIA
O my dear father! Restoration hang
Thy medicine on my lips, and let this kiss
Repair those violent harms that my two sisters
Have in thy reverence made.

KENT
                              Kind and dear princess!

CORDELIA
Had you not been their father, these white flakes
Did challenge pity of them. Was this a face
To be opposed against the warring winds?
To stand against the deep dread-bolted thunder?
In the most terrible and nimble stroke
Of quick cross lightning? To watch—poor perdu!—

Restoration . . . lips: May my kiss help restore you to health.

5

Had you not been: Even if you had not been. *Did challenge:* Would have merited. *them:* Goneril and Regan, Cordelia's two sisters. *dread-bolted:*

Cordelia, frightened to be seen by her father, starts to leave.

The Female Narrator urges her to remain with him.

Lear is helped to his feet and led to the center of the stage by Cordelia and Kent (the Male Narrator).

Cordelia kneels before her father.

Lear kneels before her.

With this thin helm? Mine enemy's dog,
Though he had bit me, should have stood that night
Against my fire. And wast thou fain, poor father,
To hovel thee with swine and rogues forlorn,
In short and musty straw? Alack, alack,
'Tis wonder that thy life and wits at once
Had not concluded all. He wakes; speak to him.
FEMALE NARRATOR
Madam, do you; 'tis fittest.
CORDELIA
How does my royal lord? How fares your majesty?
LEAR
You do me wrong to take me out o' th'grave:
Thou art a soul in bliss, but I am bound
Upon a wheel of fire, that mine own tears
Do scald like molten lead.
CORDELIA
                    Sir, do you know me?
LEAR
You are a spirit, I know. When did you die?
CORDELIA
Still, still, far wide.
FEMALE NARRATOR
He's scarce awake; let him alone awhile.
LEAR
Where have I been? Where am I? Fair daylight?
I am mightily abused. I should e'en die with pity
To see another thus. I know not what to say.
I will not swear these are my hands. Let's see,
I feel this pin prick. Would I were assured
Of my condition!
CORDELIA
                    O, look upon me, sir,
And hold your hand in benediction o'er me.
No, sir, you must not kneel.
LEAR
                    Pray, do not mock me.
I am a very foolish fond old man,
Fourscore and upward, not an hour more nor less;
And to deal plainly,
I fear I am not in my perfect mind.
Methinks I should know you, and know this man,

dreadful. *perdu:* a soldier assigned to a dangerous post. *helm:* helmet (i.e., Lear's thinning hair). *Against:* In front of. *fain:* glad (under the circumstances). *To hovel thee:* i.e., Seek shelter in a hovel (open shed). *concluded all:* come to an end completely.
20

wheel of fire: instrument of torture.

25

wide: i.e., not yet fully conscious.

30 *e'en:* even.
thus: in such a miserable condition.

35
o'er: over.

Fourscore: Eighty years old.

this man: Kent, Lear's

Cordelia holds Lear in her arms as she helps him rise.

The Female Narrator speaks to all the males (and especially to the Male Narrator).
Music begins to play, as in the first dance sequence. The men go to the women now, as if to
their original dancing partners. Their attitudes have been changed by the long night's events:
The men are warm and admiring now.
Don Pedro speaks to Hero.

Romeo to Juliet.

Bertram to another man, then to Helena.

Benedick to Beatrice.

Romeo to Juliet.

A sense of renewal spreads among the couples. They have been through a difficult, emotional

Yet I am doubtful: for I am mainly ignorant
What place this is, and all the skill I have
Remembers not these garments; nor I know not
Where I did lodge last night. Do not laugh at me;
For, as I am a man, I think this lady
To be my child Cordelia.

CORDELIA
               And so I am, I am.

FEMALE NARRATOR
When would you, my lord, or you, or you,
Have found the ground of study's excellence
Without the beauty of a woman's face?

DON PEDRO
With everything that pretty is,
My lady sweet, arise,
Arise, arise.

ROMEO
Happily met, my lady and my wife.

BERTRAM
O, here is the lady that I sent for. Welcome, fair one! Is't not a
goodly presence?

BENEDICK
She's a gallant lady!

DON PEDRO
Be that you are; that is, a woman: the honest woman, the modest wife, the virtuous creature.

BENEDICK
For when a world of men
Could not prevail with all their oratory,
Yet hath a woman's kindness overruled.

BERTRAM
Where is any author in the world
Teaches such beauty as a woman's eye?

BENEDICK
I know that a woman is a dish for the gods.

ROMEO
Thou, Julia, thou hast metamorphised me!

BERTRAM
A fine woman! a fair woman! a sweet woman!

MALE NARRATOR
I see our wars
Will turn into a peaceful comic sport

trusted friend. mainly:
completely.

50

ground: foundation, funda-
mental principle.

55

60

that you are: that which
you are.

65

70

night together, and they have reached a new sense of harmony and understanding between the sexes. The couples are dancing and kissing lightly as they exit stage right, left, and up center. One woman remains onstage, sadly neglected, till a musician crosses the stage on his way home. She runs to him, grabs him by the arm, and walks off with him. The Male Narrator bids goodnight to the departing couples, then to the audience. He starts to leave, then sees the Female Narrator standing alone. He moves toward her, stops himself, then speaks. She gives him an admonishing look. They laugh together, then exit arm in arm.

Black out.

When ladies crave to be encountered with.
Good night, ladies; good night, sweet ladies!
Good night, good night!   75
Did not I dance with you in Brabant once?

Commentary

For page numbers to individual scenes, please see List of Scenes

Each scene in our playscript has two overlapping identities: its meaning in the context of its original play and its revised purpose within the new context of *Shakespeare's Women*. In some cases, these interpretations will be identical; in others, the scene's use in *Shakespeare's Women* will be slightly different from its intent in Shakespeare's original. This commentary section will, therefore, discuss the scenes both as Shakespeare envisioned them and as we make use of them within our revised narrative.

Act I: Frailty, Thy Name is Woman

ACT I of *Shakespeare's Women* begins at a dance, where the play's two Narrators, a man and a woman, meet each other. He tries unsuccessfully to pick her up, and she rejects him scornfully. After her abrupt exit, the stage is filled with a succession of men from different plays who have had unhappy relationships with women: Benedick bemoans his treatment by Beatrice; Othello indicts Desdemona; Egeus complains about his daughter, Hermia; Hamlet rails against his mother; and Proteus laments his love for Julia. Next, several couples enter from the ballroom; in each pair of lovers, the man receives disdainful treatment from the woman: Hero and Don Pedro, Margaret and Balthasar, Ursula and Antonio, and Beatrice and Benedick. Outraged by these demonstrations of female cruelty, the Male Narrator offers to show the Female Narrator a number of longer scenes from Shakespeare's plays to prove his contention that women are indeed characterized by frailty, anger, and infidelity.

The first scene presented by the Male Narrator is taken from act I, scene ii of *King Lear*, in which the aged king divides his lands and revenues among his three grown daughters. Lear has ruled Britain for all of his adult life and has become accustomed to the pomp and ceremony that accompany his high position. He had decided, therefore, to abdicate the throne in a formal, elaborate courtly ceremony during which each of his three daughters must publicly proclaim her love for him. He will then divide the kingdom among the three accordingly as a reward for their love. As this scene begins, Cordelia's two older sisters, Goneril and Regan, have each finished long and hypocritical speeches in praise of their father. When Lear turns to Cordelia, his shy and soft-spoken youngest daughter, she is unable (or unwilling) to provide the same courtly flattery offered by her sisters. As a result, Lear disowns her in a fit of anger and embarrassment. Although the Male Narrator clearly sees Cordelia's action as a negative example of female disobedience, this scene begins *Shakespeare's Women* on an ironic note: Cordelia, like many of the women presented in act I of this play, has an inner strength and honesty that make her much more admirable than culpable.

The Male Narrator next introduces a scene from *Hamlet* (III.iv) involving Hamlet and his mother, Gertrude. At this point in the play, Hamlet knows that his father has been murdered by Hamlet's uncle, Claudius, who subsequently married Gertrude only a brief time after the death of her first husband. Bitter and angry, the young man confronts his mother with her "incestuous" behavior, rails against the indecent speed of her remarriage, and compares Claudius unfavorably with Gertrude's former husband. Although much fascinating scholarly debate has been devoted to Gertrude's relationship with Claudius and to Hamlet's intense reaction to her remarriage, at least one conclusion is clear: Both Hamlet and the Male Narrator find Gertrude's actions highly reprehensible.

This scene pitting mother against son dovetails into the next, from *Measure for Measure* (III.i), in which a young man and his sister argue over a matter of life or death. Claudio has been convicted of "fornication" (impregnating his fiancée prior to their marriage), which is a crime punishable by death in Vienna. Attempting to save him, his sister, a chaste young woman named Isabella who is about to become a nun, pleads with Angelo, the Lord Deputy, who alone has the power to reduce Claudio's sentence. In a gro-

tesque turn of events, Angelo propositions Isabella and offers the
woman her brother's freedom in return for her virginity. In this
scene, Isabella explains Angelo's obscene proposal to Claudio and
recoils violently at her brother's request that she go through with
the bargain in order to save his life. "Is't not a kind of incest," she
asks, "to take life / From thine own sister's shame?" Because of her
religious beliefs, Isabella reasons that committing such a sin on
earth would condemn her to everlasting death in hell.

Moving from this seemingly cold and insensitive young woman,
the Male Narrator next presents a scene from the delightful *A Midsummer Night's Dream* (II.i), which chronicles the unrequited love
of Helena for Demetrius. At the start of this comedy, four young
Athenians set out for the woods in order to escape the tyranny of
life in the city: Hermia, in love with Lysander; Lysander, who loves
Hermia; Demetrius, who also loves Hermia; and Helena, who loves
Demetrius. In this scene, Demetrius has followed Hermia and Lysander into the woods, while Helena has followed Demetrius. Although he scorns her, Helena still dotes on Demetrius and follows
him doggedly. Her steadfast devotion to her man becomes an ironic
compliment to her sex despite the Male Narrator's obvious view of
her as a silly, fawning woman.

Moving from one female type to another, we next meet the famous Kate from *The Taming of the Shrew* (II.i). She is one of two
daughters of Baptista Minola, a wealthy landowner in Padua.
Bianca, the youngest, adopts a sweet, docile disposition, while Kate,
her elder sister, is infamous for her angry, shrewish behavior. The
father resolves not to marry off the younger till a husband can be
found for Kate—a prospect that confounds Bianca's many suitors
till they locate a rather brash fellow, Petruchio, who is initially interested in wooing Kate because of her father's money. In this classic scene, Kate and Petruchio confront each other for the first time,
each alternating between extremes of witty wordplay, physical violence, genuine sensual attraction, and raw sexual energy. In Kate, as
in other women presented so far by the Male Narrator, the initial
appearance gives way to a far different reality beneath: Her reputed
shrewishness turns to intellectual curiosity, excitement, and then
emotional involvement in the wake of Petruchio's unconventional
behavior.

Following Kate and Petruchio onstage are two interesting characters from *The Merchant of Venice* (I.ii)—Portia, a wealthy young woman, and Nerissa, her witty maid. They are lamenting a provision in Portia's father's will that forbids her daughter from marrying unless one of her suitors chooses correctly from among three similar caskets: one of gold, another of silver, and a third of lead. In this fast-moving, humorous scene, Nerissa names her mistress' various suitors, and Portia describes each one in scornful, comic detail. Under the facade of this venial gossip, however, lurks a darker, less Christian side of Portia that seems to surface later in her persecution of the Jewish moneylender, Shylock. In this scene, though, the Male Narrator is content simply to present Portia as a giddy, crafty female "curbed by the will of a dead father."

After a brief narrative bridge, we shift to another comic scene—this one from Shakespeare's beloved *Twelfth Night* (I.v)—in which we meet Viola, a bright, attractive young woman who has been shipwrecked on the coast of Illyria. Forced by necessity to seek her fortune in this strange land, she disguises herself as a boy and joins the service of the wealthy Duke Orsino. Viola soon falls secretly in love with her new master, then finds herself in the uncomfortable position of being sent as a love emissary between Orsino and the Lady Olivia. In this scene, Viola (still in disguise) travels to Olivia's mansion, where she meets Malvolio, Olivia's pompous steward, and Maria, her maid. Orsino's declaration of love is soon rejected by Olivia, who seems to take more of an interest in Viola's masculine appearance than she did in the Duke's proposal. In a play so preoccupied with role reversals and sexual identity, Olivia's attraction to Viola brings a different aspect of femininity to *Shakespeare's Women*, and appears to support the Male Narrator's claim that men are habitually abused by women.

This scene from *Twelfth Night* is followed immediately by Sonnet 61, a vivid description of jealousy in love, which is delivered by the Male Narrator out of his frustration with the women he has encountered this evening. Acting the role of Leontes in *The Winter's Tale* (III.ii), the Male Narrator chooses his wife, Hermione, as the target of his rage and accuses her of two heinous crimes: adultery and conspiracy to murder her husband. Surrounded by her male accusers, Hermione offers a long and impassioned defense of her innocence. Her trial, in effect, serves as an emblem of the extent to which women have been on trial during the entire first act of *Shakespeare's Women*. Like her female counterparts in other plays, she acquits herself well of the charges against her. Most of the examples of culpable females set forth by the Male Narrator, in fact, have proved themselves to be honorable and virtuous by their behavior in these scenes. The Male Narrator's final line, "Frailty, thy name is woman," is thus an ironic coda to the first act of this play and suggests that female weakness, like beauty, often exists principally in the mind of the beholder.

Act II: Her Infinite Variety

ACT II of *Shakespeare's Women* begins in the early hours of the morning. The party has ended, though the guests still remain—each one looking more tired and disheveled than the next. As the Male Narrator staggers onstage, he is met by a litany of voices defending women. The Female Narrator comes onstage and declares, "Now is my turn to speak." Urged on by the chorus of females, she promises to present her view of Shakespeare's women that illustrates their "infinite variety."

The first scene she introduces, taken from *As You Like It* (III.ii), brings onstage Rosalind, one of Shakespeare's most famous heroines. Like Viola, whom we met earlier, Rosalind is masquerading as a boy for her safety. Alone in the Forest of Arden with Orlando, a man she secretly fancies, Rosalind offers to remedy his love-sick behavior by tutoring him about love. "I would cure you," she says, "if you would but call me 'Rosalind' and come every day . . . to woo me." The Female Narrator obviously admires Rosalind's strength of purpose and skill in deceiving Orlando, whom the heroine later marries.

We next meet Helena, from *All's Well That Ends Well,* who appears in two successive scenes from that play. In the first, I.i, she defends herself admirably against Parolles, a rakish young man who attempts to make her give up her old-fashioned notion of virginity. Virgins, he argues, can never bring forth girl children (whom he calls "future virgins"); they are, therefore, "enemies" to virginity because they will never give birth to it. The following scene, II.v, brings together Helena and Bertram, a noble young gentleman who has been forced to marry her against his will. In this strained meeting between the two, Bertram, who is angry and disdainful, tells the obedient Helena that he must leave her immediately.

Helena's example of steadfast devotion gives way to a more fragile and unstable image of female virtue as we encounter Ophelia in two scenes from *Hamlet*. In II.i, she explains Hamlet's odd behavior to Polonius, her overbearing, meddling father, who misinterprets the prince's actions as love-madness. In III.i, we see this irrational behavior in action as Hamlet, alone with Ophelia, accuses her unjustly of representing all the major sins and follies womankind has been charged with over the centuries. Ophelia still senses that Hamlet loves her, however, and she prays aloud for the return of his sanity. After Hamlet's angry exit, Ophelia bemoans in soliloquy the loss of her love and the degeneration of Hamlet's mind.

Following Ophelia's departure, Portia appears and delivers her famous "quality of mercy" speech from *The Merchant of Venice* (IV.i), in which she urges Shylock, the Jewish moneylender, to release the merchant Antonio from repaying his "bond" of a pound of flesh. Portia's depiction of feminine strength and Christian mercy shifts in the next scene to the formidable presence of Lady Macbeth, a woman of indomitable courage. In this scene from the beginning of the play (I.vii), Lady Macbeth encourages her husband to kill Duncan, the King of Scotland, who is a guest in their castle. Since Macbeth is next in line to the throne, Duncan's death will bring him the crown and untold wealth. The shrewd and calculating manner in which Lady Macbeth manipulates her husband offers an intriguing commentary on male-female sexual inversion in this play, the force of prophecy, and the power of evil in life.

A poignant song from *Twelfth Night*, "O Mistress Mine," leads us from the sweetness and brevity of love into the bitter unhappiness of a complex, heartrending scene from *Richard III* (IV.iv). As the evening has progressed into the early morning hours, the sense of despair has deepened as a result of the misunderstandings between men and women at the party. Three noble women mourn the sorrows of death: Queen Elizabeth, wife to King Edward IV and mother to Edward, Prince of Wales, and Richard, Duke of York (both murdered by Richard III); Margaret, widow of King Henry VI, now a pitiful hag who speaks horrible prophecies; and the Duchess of York, mother of Edward IV, Clarence, and Gloucester (who later becomes Richard III). In this scene, the three women grieve through "keening": a stately lamentation for the dead delivered in loud, wailing voices. As the mourning continues, in quieter, more hushed tones, the Queen from *Richard II* appears with her Lady-in-Waiting (III.iv), and the two of them discuss her sorrow over the impending deposition of her husband, the king, by the usurper Bolingbroke.

The next woman presented by the Female Narrator is Desdemona, from the tragedy *Othello,* who sinks into confusion and profound despair in two successive scenes from that play. In the first, IV.ii, she asks the treacherous Iago for help in regaining the favor of her husband, Othello, who incorrectly believes his wife has been unfaithful to him. The second, IV.iii, introduces Emilia, Desdemona's faithful servant and confidant, whose worldly, matter-of-fact attitude toward sex and marriage contrasts sharply with Desdemona's naïve innocence and trusting spirit. In this second scene, Emilia helps her mistress prepare herself physically for bed and emotionally for the return of her jealous husband.

The sad strains of Desdemona's "Willow" song and the young woman's desperate plight seem suddenly to invigorate the Female Narrator. Just as the Male Narrator took on the role of Leontes at the end of the first act of *Shakespeare's Women,* now the Female Narrator, in the climactic scene of this play, becomes the vibrant and high-spirited Cleopatra, Queen of Egypt, who holds every man at the party in her power. This classic scene from *Antony and Cleopatra* (II.v) pits the passionate "serpent of the Nile" against a lowly and nervous Roman messenger who must bring her news of Antony's marriage to Octavia, Caesar's sister. Enraged by his report, Cleopatra threatens to have the trembling messenger "whipped with wire and stewed in brine, / Smarting in ling'ring pickle" for bringing such a loathsome message. "Though it be honest," she finally says defiantly, "it is never good / To bring bad news."

Immediately following this scene is another in which Cleopatra is described by three Romans—Maecenas, Enobarbus, and Agrippa— in the most sensual, adoring terms possible (II.ii). The central speech by Enobarbus, well known to all lovers of Shakespeare, begins with an account of her barge, which "Burnt on the water . . . like a burnished throne," and ends with an admiring look at the lady herself: "Other women cloy / The appetites they feed, but she makes hungry / Where most she satisfies." In her own way, Cleopatra embodies all the various vices and virtues, triumphs and tragedies of the entire range of females we have met in *Shakespeare's Women.* She is womanhood itself: "Age cannot wither her, nor custom stale / Her infinite variety."

The Female Narrator's defense of women has reached an important climax in her portrayal of Cleopatra, and all that remains in *Shakespeare's Women* is to bring together the men and women of the play into some kind of joyful resolution. This is accomplished in the last two scenes presented by the actors, which bring union and harmony out of the discord between the sexes. After Sonnet 130, which urges honest, unembellished praise of womankind, we are introduced to Shakespeare's most famous lovers, Romeo and Juliet. In this scene from early in the play (II.ii), Romeo, having just met Juliet at a masked ball given by her family, courageously climbs over her garden wall and speaks to her as she gazes out her balcony window. The lines that follow present some of the purest, most beautiful poetry ever written. In *Romeo and Juliet,* the love (and death) of these two young people ends the feud between their families and brings hope and reconciliation to their world. Similarly, in *Shakespeare's Women,* the positive image of these two famous lovers helps to rejoin the warring male and female factions in the play.

The final scene in *Shakespeare's Women,* which ends appropriately as it began, is taken from *King Lear* (IV.vii), when Cordelia is reunited with her aged father. Since her rejection in act I of that play, Cordelia has been to France and returned with an army to defend her father's claim to the throne. During that time, Lear has been cruelly turned away by Goneril and Regan and forced to wander naked in the howling storm. Accompanied only by a trusted servant (Kent), a fool, and a madman, Lear comes to terms with his own humanity and mortality as he fights the elements. In this scene, Lear has been taken to safety, and he has slept soundly for the first time in many days. As he awakens, Cordelia greets him lovingly. Their reconciliation and the exquisite lines of poetry that follow serve as an emblem that brings together all the different sets of lovers in *Shakespeare's Women:* Romeo and Juliet, Bertram and Helena, Benedick and Beatrice, and the Male Narrator and Female Narrator. At the conclusion of the play, the many characters join together in celebration of Shakespeare's women and their regenerative effects upon all of mankind.

Music
OH! WILLOW, WILLOW, WILLOW!

Lento ed espressivo

A poor soul sat sigh-ing by a sy-ca-more tree, Sing wil-low, wil-low, wil-low! With his hand in his bos-om, and his head up-on his knee! Oh! wil-low, wil-low, wil-low,

wil-low, Oh! wil-low, wil-low, wil-low, wil-low, My gar-land shall

be, Sing, all a green wil - low, wil - low, wil-low,

wil-low, Ah! me, the green wil - low my gar-land must be.

"O MISTRESS MINE"

O Mis-tress mine, Where are you roam-ing? O Mis-tress mine,

Where   are   you   roam-ing? O   stay   and   hear

Your true love's com-ing, That can sing   both high and low:

Trip no fur - ther, pret - ty sweet - ing,

Jour - ney's end in lov - ers' meet - ing

Ev - e - ry wise man's son doth know.

List of Scenes

Suggested Reading

Brown, Ivor. *The Women in Shakespeare's Life*. London: Morgan-Grampian books, 1968.

Camden, Charles Carroll. *The Elizabethan Woman*. Houston: Elsevier Press, 1952.

Cook, Ann Jennalie. *Women in Shakespeare*. London: Harrap Press, 1980.

Dash, Irene G. *Wooing, Wedding, and Power: Women in Shakespeare's Plays*. New York: Columbia University Press, 1981.

Dusinberre, Juliet S. *Shakespeare and the Nature of Women*. New York: Harper and Row, 1975.

Fraser, Antonia. *The Weaker Vessel*. New York: Alfred A. Knopf, 1984.

French, Marilyn. *Shakespeare's Division of Experience*. New York: Summit Books, 1981.

Heilbrun, Carolyn G. *Toward a Recognition of Androgyny*. New York: Harper and Row, 1973.

Hunter, R. G. *Shakespeare and the Comedy of Forgiveness*. New York: Columbia University Press, 1965.

Jardine, Lisa. *Still Harping on Daughters: Women and Drama in the Age of Shakespeare*. Brighton, Sussex, England: Harvester Press, 1983.

Kahn, Coppelia. *Man's Estate: Masculine Identity in Shakespeare*. Berkeley: University of California Press, 1981.

Kanner, Barbara, ed. *The Women of England from Anglo-Saxon Times to the Present*. London: Shoe String Press, 1979.

Lenz, Carolyn, R., G. Greene, and C. T. Neeley, eds. *The Woman's Part: Feminist Criticism of Shakespeare*. Champaign: University of Illinois Press, 1980.

Maclean, Ian. *The Renaissance Notion of Woman*. Cambridge: Cambridge University Press, 1980.

Morewedge, Rosemarie T. *The Role of Woman in the Middle Ages*. Albany: State University of New York Press, 1975.

Novy, Marianne L. *Love's Argument: Gender Relations in Shakespeare*. Chapel Hill: University of North Carolina Press, 1984.

O'Faolain, Julia, and Lauro Martines, eds. *Not in God's Image: A History of Women in Europe from the Greeks to the Nineteenth Century*. London: Harper and Row, 1979.

Richmond, Hugh. *Shakespeare's Sexual Comedy*. New York: Bobbs-Merrill, 1971.

Rogers, Katherine M. *The Troublesome Helpmate: A History of Misogyny in Literature*. Seattle: University of Washington Press, 1966.

Simon, Joan. *Education and Society in Tudor England*. Cambridge: Cambridge University Press, 1966.

Stenton, Doris M. *The English Woman in History*. New York: Schocken Books, 1977.

Stone, Lawrence. *The Family, Sex, and Marriage in England, 1500–1800*. London: Harper and Row, 1977.

Stuard, Susan M., ed. *Women in Medieval Society*. Philadelphia: University of Pennsylvania Press, 1976.

Utley, F. L. *The Crooked Rib: An Analytical Index to the Argument about Women in English and Scots Literature to the End of the Year 1568*. Columbus: Ohio State University Press, 1944.

Woodbridge, Linda. *Women and the English Renaissance: Literature and the Nature of Womankind, 1540–1620*. Champaign: University of Illinois Press, 1984.